SpringerBriefs in Law

For further volumes:
http://www.springer.com/series/10164

Etienne de Lhoneux · Christos A. Vassilopoulos

The European Stability Mechanism Before the Court of Justice of the European Union

Comments on the Pringle Case

Springer

Etienne de Lhoneux
Secretariat General/Legal Department
Banque Centrale du Luxembourg
Luxembourg

Christos A. Vassilopoulos
Legal Department
Banque Centrale du Luxembourg
Luxembourg

ISSN 2192-855X ISSN 2192-8568 (electronic)
ISBN 978-3-319-01477-7 ISBN 978-3-319-01478-4 (eBook)
DOI 10.1007/978-3-319-01478-4
Springer Cham Heidelberg New York Dordrecht London

Library of Congress Control Number: 2013946310

Printed on acid-free paper

Springer is part of Springer Science+Business Media (www.springer.com)

Contents

Abbreviations

CDE	Cahiers de droit européen
CFCMLR/RTDF	Corporate Finance and Capital Law Review/Revue Trimestrielle de Droit Financier
CJEL	Columbia Journal of European Law
CJEU/ ECJ	Court of Justice of the European Union/European Court of Justice
CMLRev	Common Market Law Review
DCDSI	Diritto comunitario e degli scambi internazionali
DVBl	Deutsches Verwaltungsblatt
EC	European Communities
ECB	European Central Bank
ECFLR	European Company and Financial Law Review
ECR	European Court Report
EFSF	European Financial Stabilization Facility
EFSM	European Financial Stabilization Mechanism
ELR	European Law Review
EMU	Economic and Monetary Union
ESCB	European System of Central Banks
ESM	European Stability Mechanism
EU	European Union
EuR	Europarecht
Europe	Revue Europe
EuZW	Europäische Zeitschrift für Wirtschaftsrecht
EWS	Europäisches Wirtschafts- und Steuerrecht
GCEU/CFI	General Court of the European Union/Court of Fist Instance
GDAmm	Giornale di Dirittto amministrativo
GLJ	German Law Journal
ICLQ	International and Comparative Law Quaterly
JCP	Jurisclasseur périodique (Semaine juridique)
JDI (Clunet)	Journal du droit International
JRP	Journal für Rechtspolitk
MJ	Maastricht Journal
NCB	National Central Bank
NVwZ	Neue Zeitschrift für Verwaltungsrecht

Nyr	Decisions of the European Union judicature not yet reported
OJ	Official Journal of the European Communities/European Union
ÖJZ	Österreichische Juristen-Zeitung
OMT	Outright Monetary Transactions
Para(s)	Paragraph(s) of the judgment of the CJEU or of the Articles of the Treaty on the European Union and the Treaty on the Functioning of the European Union
RAE/LEA	Revue des affaires européennes/Law and European affairs
RCGI	Rivista della cooperazione giuridica internazionale
RDUE	Revue du droit de l'Union européenne
RGDIP	Revue Générale de droit international public
RMCUE	Revue du Marché commun et de l'Union européenne
RTDE	Revue trimestrielle de droit européen
SGP	Stability and Growth Pact
SMP	Securities Market Program
STACOG Treaty	Stability Coordination and Governance Treaty
TEU	Treaty on European Union
TFEU	Treaty on the Functioning of the European Union
ZEuS	Zeitschrift für Europarechtliche Studien
ZWBR	Zeitschrift für Wirtschafts- und Bankrecht

Chapter 1
Introduction: Background

The Pringle case is to be welcomed, the Court of Justice of the European Union (CJEU or the Court), in its full composition, thoroughly examined the core provisions of the European Monetary Union (EMU) (Articles 121–127 Treaty on the Functioning of the European Union or TFEU).

In the past the CJEU had the opportunity to interpret exclusively the provisions of the economic pillar of the EMU. In 2004, the Court took position on the first Stability and Growth Pact (SGP)[1] in the case Commission v Council[2] regarding the particular procedure of excessive deficits (now Article 126 TFEU) vis-à-vis some Member States (Germany and France). The CJEU pointed out the peculiarities of this procedure and put in evidence the weaknesses of the mechanisms provided for in the Treaties. The issues of this litigation were the scope of application of Article 126 TFEU and the interpretation of the main rules of the SGP. The assessment and conclusions developed in such occasion were limited[3] and a debate started concerning the need to reinforce the legal framework of the rules regarding the budgetary discipline of the Member States and the necessity to adapt the SGP.

The first reaction in that respect was the amendment of the SGP in 2005[4] shortly after the judgment Commission v Council, mentioned above. Despite the strengthening of the legal framework of the SGP in its preventive and corrective arms as

---

[1] Council Regulation (EC) n°1466/97 of 7 July 1997 on the strengthening of the surveillance of budgetary positions and the surveillance and coordination of economic policies (OJ L 209, p. 1) and Council Regulation (EC) n°1467/97 of 7 July 1997 on speeding up and clarifying the implementation of the excessive deficit procedure (OJ L 209, p. 6).

[2] Case C-27/04, *Commission v Council*, [2004] ECR I-6649.

[3] See Bandilla (2005), pp. 538–549 sp. 541; Chaltiel (2004), pp. 509–514, sp. 512; Häde (2004), pp. 750–764, sp. 752; Henseler (2004), pp. 541–558, sp. 554; Maher (2004), pp. 831–841, sp. 833; Presutti (2005), pp. 65–81, sp. 77–78.

[4] Council Regulation (EC) n°1055/2005 of 27 June 2005 amending Regulation (EC) n°1466/97 on the strengthening of the surveillance of budgetary positions and the surveillance and coordination of economic policies, (OJ L 174, p. 1) and Council Regulation (EC) n°1056/2005 of 27 June 2005 amending Regulation (EC) n°1467/97 on speeding up and clarifying the implementation of the excessive deficit procedure (OJ L 174, p. 5).

E. de Lhoneux and C. A. Vassilopoulos, *The European Stability Mechanism Before the Court of Justice of the European Union*, SpringerBriefs in Law,
DOI: 10.1007/978-3-319-01478-4_1, © The Author(s) 2014

put in place in 2005, the Member States continued not to tackle their deficits adequately.

Considering that the deepening of the financial crisis led to a severe deterioration of the borrowing conditions in several Member States, particularly in Greece, in May 2010 Regulation n°407/2010[5] was adopted establishing the *European Financial Stabilisation Mechanism (EFSM)*, based on Article 122 para 2 TFEU. This Regulation established the conditions and procedures under which European financial assistance could be granted to a Member State which is experiencing or is seriously threatened by a severe economic or financial disturbance caused by exceptional occurrences beyond its control.

During the same period (June 2010), with the establishment of the *European Financial Stabilisation Facility (EFSF)*, a *"société anonyme"* incorporated in Luxembourg, financial support was provided to euro area Member States in difficulties caused by exceptional circumstances, with the aim of safeguarding the financial stability of the euro area was a whole and of its Member States. The EFSF was entitled to raise money by issuing financial instruments or by entering into financing arrangements with its shareholders or third parties. Liabilities of the EFSF were guaranteed by some or all of its shareholders or otherwise collateralized or could benefit from credit support mechanisms. In that respect, the EFSF signed with the euro area Members States the EFSF Framework Agreement.

The euro indicators showed a clear deterioration of the financial situation in the Euro zone during 2010. In the euro area the government debt to GDP ratio increased from 79.3 % at the end of 2009 to 85.1 % at the end of 2010.[6]

Member States decided to react at different levels. Firstly, they decided to amend the European Treaties and to use for the first time the simplified revision procedure provided for in Article 48 para 6 of the Treaty on the European Union (TEU) in order to envisage the possibility to establish a permanent stability mechanism. On 25 March 2011, the European Council adopted Decision 2011/199 with regard to a stability mechanism for Member States whose currency is the euro (European Council Decision 2011/199)[7] adding a third paragraph to Article 136 TFEU which reads as follows:

> The Member States whose currency is the euro may establish a stability mechanism to be activated if indispensable to safeguard the stability of the euro area as a whole. The granting of any required financial assistance under the mechanism will be made subject to strict conditionality.

This provision does not mention expressly the possibility for the Member States to conclude an international treaty in order to "activate this mechanism". However, the wording of this provision suggests implicitly that Member States could undertake actions taking the form of an international agreement.

---

[5] Council Regulation (EU) n°407/2010 of 11 May 2010 establishing a European financial stabilisation mechanism (OJ L 118, p. 1).

[6] EUROSTAT, Press release euro indicators, 60/2011, 26 April 2011.

[7] OJ 2011 L 91, p. 1.

Secondly, the SGP was modified a third time[8] in order to reinforce the surveillance of budgetary positions. Indeed, it is considered that the second amendment to the SGP in 2005 did not confer on the Council the necessary powers to effectively examine Member States' programs concerning their budgetary discipline.[9]

Furthermore, supplementary EU measures were adopted which constitute today the new framework aiming at an effective budgetary discipline.[10] The SGP was complemented, on one hand, by three regulations concerning respectively the enforcement of budgetary surveillance in the euro area, the mechanisms concerning the prevention and correction of macroeconomic imbalances in the euro area and the prevention and correction of macroeconomic imbalances[11] and, on the other hand, by a directive on requirements for budgetary frameworks of the Member States.[12]

The legal proliferation of secondary legislation in November 2011 in the field of budgetary discipline is considered by the EU institutions as the necessary way to tackle, from a legal perspective, the economic crisis inside the euro area. However, someone could argue that this intervention in secondary level legislation, "massive and complex"[13] might contribute to the general confusion about the scope of the new legal framework and its effectiveness. Despite the efforts of the EU institutions, it seems that it was necessary to take supplementary initiatives.

In that respect, the Member States decided thirdly to act unilaterally by concluding international agreements. It is really interesting to observe that the Member States decided to complete the EU legal framework composed mainly by direct effect rules by means of international agreements. This might be an indication that the relevant legal framework, shortly after its adoption in November 2011, was not perceived as the sole way to ensure an effective budgetary discipline and to reinforce the legal framework of the coordination of the economic policies of the Member States.

---

[8] Regulation (EU) n° 1175/2011 of 16 November 2011 amending Council Regulation (EC) n°1466/97 on the strengthening of the surveillance of budgetary positions and the surveillance and coordination of economic policies (OJ L 306, p. 12) and Council Regulation (EU) n°1177/2011 of 8 November 2011 amending Regulation (EC) n° 1467/97 on speeding up and clarifying the implementation of the excessive deficit procedure (OJ L 306, p. 33).

[9] See Louis (2011), pp. 353–367, sp. 360; Louis (2006), pp. 85–106, sp. 101; see also, Amtenbrink and De Haan (2006), pp. 402–413, sp. 405.

[10] See Allemand and Martucci (2012), pp. 17–99, sp. 97.

[11] Regulation (EU) n°1173/2011 of the European Parliament and of the Council of 16 November 2011 on the effective enforcement of budgetary surveillance in the euro area (OJ L 306, p. 1), Regulation (EU) n°1174/2011 of the European Parliament and of the Council of 16 November 2011 on enforcement measures to correct excessive macroeconomic imbalances in the euro area (OJ L 306, p. 8) and Regulation (EU) n°1176/2011 of the European Parliament and of the Council of 16 November 2011 on the prevention and correction of macroeconomic imbalances (OJ L 306, p. 25).

[12] Council Directive 2011/85/EU of 8 November 2011 on requirements for budgetary frameworks of the Member States, (OJ L 306, p. 41).

[13] See Adamski (2012), pp. 1319–1364, sp. 1337.

Therefore, Member States of the euro area decided to establish a permanent mechanism of financial stability through the adoption of an international agreement such as the treaty establishing the European Stability mechanism (ESM Treaty or ESM) which is a continuation of the former mechanisms as confirmed by recital 1 of such Treaty according to which the ESM aims to carry out the tasks previously fulfilled by the EFSF and the EFSM. This Treaty was adopted by the seventeen euro area Member States on 2 February 2012 independently from the modification envisaged by the European Council Decision 2011/199 in Article 136 TFEU which entered into force on 1 May 2013 following completion of the ratification process in Czech Republic (that is to say on a date subsequent to the ruling of the Court).

The initial maximum lending volume of the ESM was set at 500 billion euros, including the outstanding EFSF support (recital 6 of the ESM Treaty). In its statement of 30 March 2012 and in order to improve market confidence, the Eurogroup decided that the current overall ceiling for ESM/EFSF lending was to be raised to 700 billion euros in order to allow the ESM and the EFSF to operate effectively. It was the first time that certain Member States had to pulled together such a level of financial assistance.[14] The ESM Treaty and the EFSF Framework Agreement constitute the legal instruments on the basis of which the euro area Member States decided to intervene at international level in order to put in place the appropriate mechanisms strengthening the economic pillar of the EMU.

In addition to the ESM and to the EFSF Framework Agreement, the Treaty on Stability Coordination and Governance in the EMU (STACOG Treaty), the so called "Fiscal Compact", was signed by 25 Member States during the European Council meeting on 1 and 2 March 2012. According to Article 1 of this Treaty, the Contracting Parties agreed, as Member States of the European Union, to strengthen the economic pillar of the Economic and Monetary Union by adopting a set of rules intended to foster budgetary discipline through a fiscal compact, to strengthen the coordination of economic policies and to improve the governance of the euro area, thereby supporting the achievement of the European Union objectives for sustainable growth, employment, competitiveness and social cohesion.

With their different scope, the STACOG Treaty, the EFSF Framework Agreement and the ESM Treaty were considered by the Member States as a combined system of rules fostering fiscal responsibility and solidarity within the EMU. Concerning in particular the STACOG and the ESM Treaty, this is expressly provided for in recital 5 of the ESM Treaty.

The action of the Member States aimed at strengthening the economic pillar of the EMU has covered any level of legal instruments. Indeed, firstly, it was envisaged a modification of primary European law by adding a new paragraph in Article 136 TFEU.[15] Secondly, the current secondary European legislation was amended in order to reinforce the existing SGP[16] with a new regulatory framework

---

[14] See Napolitano (2012), pp. 461–469, sp. 465.

[15] Louis (2012b), pp. 284–320, sp. 306.

[16] Louis (2012a), pp. 57–83, sp. 61.

and a supplementary focus on harmonization (3 additional regulations and Directive 2011/85/EU). Thirdly, the Member States acted outside the European Union framework with the adoption of different international agreements. In particular, the STACOG Treaty, added to the measures aiming at the reinforcement of the economic coordination of the Member States, and the ESM Treaty establishing a permanent financial stability mechanism.

The new framework presents therefore a multilevel differentiation i.e. the adoption of EU measures and intergovernmental acts and, within this latter category, three different international agreements. Indeed, the ESM and the EFSF Framework Agreement were concluded only by the euro area Member States and the STACOG Treaty by twenty-five EU Member States. Even if, in the medium term, the aim pursued by the Member States involved is probably to incorporate the common experience resulting from these treaties in the EU legal framework, at the present stage, these three agreements present a substantial differentiation in particular at an institutional level. This element still remains as one of the most fundamental differences between on the one hand the ESM Treaty and the EFSF Framework Agreement and on the other hand the STACOG Treaty despite the efforts of the Contracting Parties to present the treaties under discussion as complementary legal instruments of the EU law.

The actions of the EU institutions and the Member States did not reverse the tendencies of the economic indicators in 2012. Indeed, the government debt to GDP ratio in the euro area continued to stand at a very high level i.e. at 90.0 %. The highest ratios were recorded in Greece (150.3 %), Italy (126.1 %), Portugal (117.5 %) and Ireland (111.5 %).[17]

The option of the Member States to conclude international agreements such as the ESM Treaty, the EFSF Framework Agreement and the STACOG Treaty, without the formal involvement of the EU, had particular legal consequences. Pursuant to the constitutional law of certain Member States, these treaties as international agreements were subject to the review of the competent national courts. It is noteworthy that the decisions of constitutional courts such as the Bundesvefassungsgericht (BVG)[18] ruled in favour of the compatibility of the ESM Treaty and the STACOG Treaty with national requirements. In this decision, the Federal Constitutional Court of Germany restated its previous case law regarding the legal instruments and other measures in connection with the aid to Greece and with the euro rescue package. Importantly, the BVG decided to rule without making a reference for a preliminary ruling.

In contrast, the Supreme Court of Ireland considered necessary for the Court of justice to exercise its primary competence in order to interpret EU primary law provisions and decided to make a reference to the CJEU by way of a preliminary

[17] EUROSTAT, Press release euro indicators, 150/2012, 24 October 2012.

[18] German Federal Constitutional, (BVerfG 2-BvR 1390/12, 2-BvR 1421/12, 2-BvR 1438/12. 2-BvR 1439/12, 2-BvR 1440/12 and 2-BvE 6/12), Judgment of 12 September 2012 on the ratification of the ESM and the STACOG Treaty; Schorkopf (2012a), pp. 554–562, sp. 561; (same article in German Schorkopf (2012b), pp. 1273–1276); Wollenschläger (2012), pp. 713–719, sp. 716.

ruling on 31 July 2012. This initiative is all the more welcome as it allowed the Court to positively develop its case law on the matter, also given the political reactions and the debate concerning the organization of a referendum on the Treaties amendment related to the European Stability Mechanism.[19] The CJEU ruled on 27 November 2012 (case C-370/12) under the accelerated procedure in accordance with the relevant provisions of the Statute and of the Rules of Procedure of the Court of Justice.

Firstly, the referring national Court asked the CJEU about the validity of the European Council Decision 2011/199 adopted under Article 48 para 6 TEU. This Article, introduced in the corpus of the European Treaties with the Treaty of Lisbon, confers on the European Council the power to adopt a decision amending all or single provisions of Part Three of the TFEU, upon condition that the competences conferred on the Union in the Treaties remain unchanged. However, the main issue of the litigation before the national court was whether the European Council Decision 2011/199 falls within the sphere of EU monetary policy, that is to say an exclusive competence of the EU or, anyway, this decision unduly affects the balance of competence between the EU and Member States in relation to the economic pillar of the EMU.[20] In other words, the question was whether the European Council Decision 2011/199 could also affect provisions of Part One of the TFEU.

Secondly, it was claimed before the national judge that the ESM treaty itself, as concluded by the euro area Member States, encroaches upon the monetary policy and infringes the fundamental rules concerning the coordination of the economic policies such as provided for in the treaties. Furthermore, the referring judge requested the CJEU whether the specific competences conferred by the ESM Treaty on certain EU institutions are compatible with their functions as determined by the EU primary law and, particularly, if the Member States in general could conclude an international agreement such as the ESM Treaty in the field of the EMU without breaching the fundamental rules of the European Treaties.

In relation to the above, one should note that the Court has consistently declined its jurisdiction in the case of international agreements concluded exclusively by all or a group of Member States without the participation of the European Union.[21] If the Court had followed strictly its case law on the matter, it would have needed to decline its jurisdiction, the ESM treaty having been concluded exclusively by the Member States forming the euro area. It is perhaps on the basis of this justification that the BVG did not make a reference for a preliminary ruling to the Court. In that context, given the political value of the issues at stake, the Court pragmatically accepted to rule on the preliminary ruling of the Supreme Court of Ireland and this was done on the basis of a new legal doctrine as further explained below.

---

[19] See Barrett (2011), pp. 152–155.

[20] Häde (2012), pp. 421–439.

[21] See for instance Case C-533/08, *TNT Express,* [2010] ECR I-4107, paras 60 and 61 and Case C-132/09, *Commission v Belgium,* [2010] ECR I-8695, para 43 cited also by the Court in the Pringle case, para 78.

Despite the authoritative interpretation provided by the Court in the field of monetary and economic policy, it should be critically pointed out that the Court makes continuous reference to its previous case law, even if the procedural aspects related to Article 48 para 6 TFEU and the substantive issues at stake are entirely new (i.e. ERTA case as well as Opinion 1/91, Opinion 1/00, Unièn de Pequeños Agricultores case etc.). One could note that the Court, as a high jurisdiction, could have developed a completely new legal doctrine, particularly as this was the first time after the 2004 enlargement that the Court ruled in full composition on a preliminary ruling procedure[22] and also considering the importance of the dispute.[23]

While the Pringle judgment may give rise to some critical observations, it is certain that it is to be welcomed as a new step in the case law of the CJEU which shows that the Court's role in similar issues is likely to be increasingly important in the coming years. For instance, issues regarding the oversight policy of the ECB have already been brought before the European judicature,[24] as well as litigation regarding the eligibility of marketable debt instruments issued or fully guaranteed by a Member State in the context of a debt exchange offer.[25] Recently, also the litigation regarding the Eurosystem's outright transactions in secondary sovereign bond markets has been brought before the Court.[26] As a result, a Court judging on financial and economic issues will likely be in need of specialized technical expertise in this field, and of specific procedural rules to carry out its tasks.

It must be observed that since the establishment of the CJEU, the legal framework of the European Union has significantly evolved. As it is generally recognized, with its case law, the Court has always played a substantial role in the establishment of the EU legal order. Today, however, the evolution of the EU and its new physiognomy will gradually require for financial and economic issues to be addressed by a judicature with specialized technical tools. In this respect, it can be observed that most of the litigation in these fields is settled via alternative dispute resolution systems. This indeed prompts the question whether the specific issues related to the EMU should be assessed by a specialized EU judicial body. This is all the more necessary considering the current developments in the field of the Banking Union, particularly prudential supervision and resolution.

The need for a specific CJEU competence, more closely related to the arbitration model, is confirmed also by the choice made by Member States in the context of the ESM treaty (recital 16 and Article 37) and the STACOG Treaty (Article 8) conferring jurisdiction to the Court in the specific context of the review provided for in Article 273 TFEU. There is no doubt that the disputes between Member States in the peculiar context of the ESM and the fiscal compact must be solved

[22] Recently, the Court has ruled in full composition in order to deliver an Opinion (procedure of article 218§11 TFEU), which is a specific procedure laid down by the treaty (Opinion 1/09, *Draft Agreement creating a Unified Patent Litigation System,* [2011] ECR I-1145.

[23] Simon (2013), pp 17–20.

[24] Case T-496/11, *UK v ECB* and case T-45/12 *UK v ECB*.

[25] Case T-224/12, *Accorinti e.a. v ECB*.

[26] Case T-492/12, *von Storch e.o. v ECB*.

under a specific judicial regime which the Member States considered the CJEU could put in place in the framework of Article 273 TFEU. In fact, Member States decided to confer this jurisdiction on the Court despite the peculiarity characterizing the economic and banking issues. In the Pringle judgment the Court for the first time had the opportunity to interpret the regime of Article 273 TFEU, a provision which was included since the Treaty of Rome establishing the EEC.

Along the same lines, the Contracting Parties in the EFSF Framework Agreement provided that in the absence of an amicable agreement in case of a dispute between the Member States of the euro area (to the extent that it constitutes a dispute between them only), such dispute shall be submitted to the exclusive jurisdiction of the Court of Justice of the European Union (Article 16 para 2). This provision does not mention expressly that the CJEU has jurisdiction on the basis of Article 273 TFEU. However, it is only on the basis of this provision that the CJEU could resolve a dispute between the Member States concerning this agreement. It must be noted that according to the same provision of the EFSM framework Agreement in case of a dispute between one or more euro-area Member States and the EFSF, the Parties agree to submit the dispute to the exclusive jurisdiction not of the CJEU but of the Courts of the Grand Duchy of Luxembourg. This is one of the important peculiarities related to the judicial review of the EFSF.

In the light of the foregoing, the comments concerning the Pringle judgment fall within three main categories:

The first is related to the jurisdiction of the Court to examine the conditions laid out by Article 48 para 6 TEU and to interpret an agreement concluded exclusively by Member States;

The second concerns the use of the simplified revision procedure (Article 48 para 6 TEU) in the field of the EMU; in that context, the CJEU examined exclusively whether the proposed amendment of Article 136 TFEU was compatible with the European Treaties;

The third is about the question whether the ESM Treaty itself constitutes an agreement which subverts the European legal order governing the two so-called pillars of the EMU (monetary and economic) and also the fundamental rules regarding the exercise of the competences allocated to the Union. In particular the CJEU develops an in-depth interpretation of the provisions concerning the economic policy as provided for in Articles 120 TFEU to 126 TFEU; in the same context the Court examined the question whether the role allocated to the EU institutions (Commission, ECB, and the Court itself) in the framework of the ESM treaty is compatible with the powers of these institutions as defined in the European Treaties. In the same context, the Court examined finally if the conclusion of the ESM Treaty by the Member States of the Euro Area is in line with the rights guaranteed by the Charter of the Fundamental Rights of the European Union.

References

Adamski D (2012) National power games and structural failures in the European macroeconomic governance. CMLRev:1319–1364

Allemand F, Martucci F (2012) La nouvelle Gouvernance économique européenne. CDE:17–99

Amtenbrik F, De Haan J (2006) Reforming the stability and growth pact. ELR:402–413
Bandilla R (2005) Ist der Stabilitäts- und Wachstumspakt rechtlich durchsetzbar? Anmerkungen zum Urteil des Gerichtshofes in der Rechtssache Kommission/Rat (C-37/04). In: Zuleeg M, Gaitanides C, Kadelbach S, Rodriguez Iglesias GC (eds) Festschrift für Manfred Zuleeg. Nomos, Baden–Baden, pp 538–549
Barrett G (2011) The treaty amendment on the European stability mechanism: does it require a referendum in Ireland? Irish Law Times:152–155
Chaltiel F (2004) Le pacte de stabilité, entre exigences juridiques et pragmatisme politique. À propos de l'arrêt du 13 juillet 2004. RMCUE:509–514
Häde U (2004) Der EuGH und die Haushaltsdisziplin—Das Urteil vom 13.7.2004 zum Verfahren bei einem übermäßigen Defizit. EuR 2004:750–764
Häde U (2012) The Treaty of Lisbon and the Economic and Monetary Union. In: Blanke H-J, Mangiameli S (eds) The European Union after Lisbon, Constitutional basis, economic order and external action. Springer, Heidelberg, pp 421–439
Henseler P (2004) Galgenfrist für den Stabilitätspakt—Interinstitutionelle Handlungsspielräume von Rat und Kommission im Verfahren bei einem übermäßigen Defizit nach Auffassung des EuGH. ZEuS 2004:541–558
Louis J-V (2006) The Review of the Stability and Growth Pact. CMLRev:85–106
Louis J-V (2011) Editorial: Les réponses à la crise. CDE:353–367
Louis J-V (2012a) L'Union économique et monétaire de Maastricht à la crise. RAE/LEA:57–83
Louis J-V (2012b) The unexpected revision of the Lisbon treaty and the establishment of a European stability mechanism. In: Ashiagbor DC (ed) The European union after the treaty of Lisbon. Cambridge University Press, Cambridge, pp 284–320
Maher I (2004) Economic policy coordination and the European court: excessive deficits and ECOFIN discretion. ELR:831–841
Napolitano G (2012) La nuova governance economica europea: il meccanismo di stabilita ed il Fiscal Compact. GDAmm:461–469
Presutti E (2005) La Corte di giustizia e il patto di stabilità e di crescita: commento alla sentenza del 13 luglio 2004. DCDSI:65–81
Schorkopf F (2012a) Start the engines. Comment on the ESM-judgment of the German Federal Constitutional Court of 12 September 2012. MJ (Maastricht University):554–562
Schorkopf F (2012b) Startet die Maschinen: das ESM-Urteil des BVerfG vom 12.9.2012. NVwZ:1273–1276
Simon D (2013) Mécanisme européen de stabilité (MES). Europe:17-20
Wollenschläger F (2012) Völkerrechtliche Flankierung des EU-Integrationsprogramms als Herausforderung für den Europa-Artickel des Grundgesetzes (Article 23 GG). NVwZ:713–719

Chapter 2
The Jurisdiction of the Court

The issues related to the jurisdiction of the Court are highly relevant as for the first time the Court developed a specific reasoning in order to recognise its jurisdiction to interpret on the one hand international agreements concluded exclusively by Member States and, on the other, its jurisdiction concerning the examination of the simplified revision procedure.

On the basis of its traditional case law, the Court could have easily declined its jurisdiction to rule on these two issues. However, with a new type of reasoning the Court declared its jurisdiction firstly in order to interpret—in a preliminary ruling procedure—the provisions of an international agreement to which the European Union is not a contracting party and (Sect. 2.1) secondly to give preliminary ruling on the validity of the acts of EU institutions in the particular context of the simplified revision procedure as for Article 48 para 6 TEU (Sect. 2.2).

2.1 The Interpretation of International Agreements Concluded Exclusively by The EU Member States

According to the settled case law of the Court,[1] when the European Union is not a contracting party to an international agreement (such as the ESM Treaty) the Court has no jurisdiction, in principle, to interpret this Treaty in the framework of a preliminary ruling. In that respect, the Court also considered that despite the fact that a convention (e.g. Convention of 1957—Statute of the European Schools) is linked to the European Union and the functioning of its institutions, such convention concluded exclusively by the Member States does not form an integral part of European law and, therefore, the Court has no jurisdiction to interpret it. The case of the Convention on the Statute of the European Schools is significant as the Court could have based its jurisdiction on the fact that his convention is directly

[1] Case C-132/09 *Commission v Belgium*, [2010] ECR I-8695, paras 43 and 44 and the cited case law.

E. de Lhoneux and C. A. Vassilopoulos, *The European Stability Mechanism Before the Court of Justice of the European Union*, SpringerBriefs in Law,
DOI: 10.1007/978-3-319-01478-4_2,

connected to the interests of the European Union as a whole. The fact that the Court avoided even in this case to declare its jurisdiction shows the difficulty for the Court to recognise its jurisdiction in the absence of an overruling or of the establishment of a new regime of exemptions.

In that respect, it must be reminded that the Court recognized that even though an agreement was concluded exclusively by Member States, it had jurisdiction under certain circumstances. Indeed, in the TNT case the Court stated that *"it is only where and in so far as the European Union has assumed the powers previously exercised by the Member States in the field to which an international convention not concluded by the European Union applies and, therefore, the provisions of the convention have the effect of binding the European Union that the Court has jurisdiction to interpret such a convention"*.[2]

The exception above was initially formulated by the European Court of Justice in a different context in order to deal with the succession of the former European Economic Community to the obligations of its Member States deriving from their participation to the first GATT, the so-called GATT 1947[3] (International Fruit Company case).[4] In the TNT case, the Court stated expressly its jurisdiction to interpret international agreements not formally concluded by the European Union on the basis of the succession theory, an element which was the basis of the reasoning of the Court in the International Fruit Company case.

In the Pringle case, the Court had the choice to elaborate a new category of exceptions with respect to the regime of exceptions admitted in the TNT case. For instance, the Court could have grounded its jurisdiction on the fact that EU institutions such as the ECB and the Commission, and also the Court itself as EU institution, were largely involved in the ESM Treaty framework.

However given the specificities of the pending litigation, the Court preferred to justify its jurisdiction based on a different line of reasoning, namely that the question submitted by the national Court concerned the interpretation of various provisions of EU law (and not the interpretation of the ESM provisions) (para 79). In fact, the judgment concludes that the CJEU has "*jurisdiction to provide the national court with all the criteria for the interpretation of the European Union law which may enable it to asses whether the provisions of the ESM Treaty are compatible with European Union law*" (para 80).

One could argue that the Court found a new basis for its jurisdiction. In reality, however, the European case law shows that the Court applied a similar reasoning when in preliminary ruling proceedings it was invited by national courts to interpret national law. While the Court does not have jurisdiction to give a ruling on the compatibility of

---

[2] Case C-533/08, *TNT*, [2010] ECR I-4107, para 60.

[3] This version of the General Agreement on Tariffs and Trade (GATT 1947) predates the GATT concluded in the framework of World Trade Organization in 1994 (GATT 1994) in which the EEC was a contracting party (see, *Opinion 1/94, Competence of the Community to conclude international agreements concerning services and the protection of intellectual property*, [1994] ECR I-5267).

[4] Joined cases 21/72–24/72, *International Fruit Company NV and others*, [1972] ECR 1219, para 18.

national law with European Union law, according to its settled case-law, it has jurisdiction *"... to give the national court full guidance on the interpretation of European Union law in order to enable it to determine the issue of compatibility of a national measure with that law for the purposes of deciding the case before it."*[5]

For the Court, the substantial "condition" justifying its jurisdiction is the necessity to provide the national courts with criteria for the interpretation of EU law. The scope of this "condition" is very broad and is likely to grant jurisdiction to the Court in a number of cases. With this case law, the Court modifies de facto its previous tradition according to which it has not jurisdiction to interpret agreements concluded exclusively by Member States. As it results from paras 79–80, the rationale for the jurisdiction of the Court is the necessity to provide the national judge with the criteria for the interpretation of European Law.

The reasoning of the Court could eventually be critically assessed, from a different perspective, that is with regard to the remedies system provided for by the Treaties. The Court examined in the past the possibility that a Member State or a group of Member States (as it was *Open Skies*[6] litigation) could infringe EU law by entering into an international agreement. Such finding can typically be made in the context of an infringement procedure (Article 258 TFEU) in which the European Commission has a leading role. The Court did not make any comment in that respect but it seems that its position has a supplementary justification.

The ESM Treaty, as an international agreement, was subject to the review of the competent national courts and in that respect, for instance, the BVG expressed its view about the scope and content of primary law provisions such as Articles 122 TFEU, 123 TFEU and 125 TFEU.[7] In particular, the BVG developed inter alia a specific reasoning regarding the direct acquisition of debt instruments in the secondary market by the ECB without the need to invoke the intervention of the European Courts. In its judgment of 12 September 2012 on the ratification of the ESM and the STACOG Treaty, the BVG confirmed in fact its previous position regarding the interpretation of the above mentioned articles of the TFEU in its judgment concerning the Greek financial aid.[8]

Certainly one could argue that the BVG preferred not to make a reference for a preliminary ruling because the Court Justice has not in principle jurisdiction to interpret international agreements concluded by the Member States such as the ESM Treaty. In addition, it could be supported that the BVG could in any case justify its decision not to make a reference for a preliminary ruling before the CJEU in accordance with the doctrine of *"acte clair"*.

---

[5] See, inter alia, Case C-140/09, *Fallimento Traghetti del Mediterraneo SpA*, [2010] ECR I-5243, paras 23–24.

[6] See Case C-476/98, *Commission of the European Communities v Federal Republic of Germany*, [2002] ECR I-9855.

[7] See in a different context, Schmidt (2013), pp. 1–19, sp. 15.

[8] German Federal Constitutional, (*BVerfG 2-BvR 97/10, 2-BvR 1099/10 and 2-BvR 1485/10*), *Judgment* of 7 September 2011, Legal instruments and other measures in connection, with the aid to Greece and with the euro rescue package. See in that respect Dechatre (2011), pp. 303–342, sp. 323.

In the Pringle case, the Court however gave a clear answer to the national judicial authorities according to which it is for the Court to provide the national courts with the relevant criteria for the interpretation of the primary European law provisions. If the ESM treaty was to be interpreted by national courts in relation to primary law provisions, this could alter the homogeneous interpretation of EU primary law. In addition, the fact that the ESM is such a sensitive subject matter for the future of the EMU, especially during the financial crisis, together with the fact that it was for the first time question to interpret exhaustively primary law provision made the reference for a preliminary ruling quasi- imperative. This was evident for the referring judge.

In the light of these considerations, it must be pointed out that, even if the basis of the jurisdiction of the Court to interpreter the ESM Treaty deviates from its case law elaborated in this matter, notably the regime of the exceptions indicated in the TNT case, the Court preferred to remind the national judge of the importance and the function of the preliminary ruling mechanism within the EU law. Indeed, the spirit of cooperation which must prevail in the preliminary ruling procedure requires the national court for its part to have regard to the function entrusted to the Court of Justice and that in particular in relation to primary law provisions.

2.2 The Review of the Validity of the Acts of the European Council in the Particular Context of the Simplified Revision Procedure as for Article 48 para 6 TEU

In the case at glance, the reference for a preliminary ruling concerns also European Council Decision 2011/199 adopted pursuant to Article 48 para 6 TEU and amending Article 136 TFEU. Formally,[9] this decision is an act of an EU institution—the European Council—on the validity of which the CJEU has jurisdiction to give a preliminary ruling (Article 267 para 1b TFEU). It is precisely on this element that the CJEU builds the first step of its reasoning (para 31).

However, even if the European Council Decision 2011/199 is formally an act of an EU institution, this act concerns, in fact, a new provision to be added in the corpus of the European Treaties (i.e. Article 136 para 3 TFEU). Therefore, the question is whether the CJEU has the jurisdiction to asses the validity of provisions of the Treaty (primary law) in the context of a preliminary ruling, no specific procedure having been provided in this regard by the Treaties.

The Court reminds that the examination of the validity of primary law does not fall within the CJEU's jurisdiction (para 33). Nevertheless, the Court embraces a different approach and devotes four paragraphs to affirm its jurisdiction (paras 33–36).

In para 33 the Court states that after the entry into force of the Treaty of Lisbon—and the establishment of a simplified revision procedure—*"the question*

[9] Partsch and Robberecht (2013), pp. 77–89, sp. 78, point 10.

*arises whether the Court is required to ensure that the Member States, when they undertake a revision of the treaty using the simplified revision, comply with the conditions laid down by (*Article 48 para TEU)", provision which is quoted in para 34.

Paras 33–34 above suggest clearly that the context underlying European Council Decision 2011/199 amending Article 136 TFEU is very different from the context applicable to European institutions acts adopted in general framework of the European decision-making process. Nevertheless, the Court did not take into consideration this element and affirmed that *"since it is necessary that compliance with the conditions of Article 48 para 6 TEU be monitored in order to establish whether the simplified revision procedure is applicable, it falls to the CJEU, as the institution which, under the first subpara of Article 19 para 1 TEU, is to ensure that the law is observed in the interpretation and application of the Treaties, to examine the validity of a decision of the European Council based on Article 48 para 6 TEU"* (para 35). In that respect, the judgment continues stating that *"it is for the CJEU to verify first that the procedural rules laid down in this Article were followed and secondly that the amendments decided upon concern only Part there of the TFEU"* (para 36).

In sum, the jurisdiction of the Court seems to be based on two elements: firstly, on the fact that European Council Decision 2011/199 is formally an act of a European institution which, as such, and according to its case law, could be subject to a reference for a preliminary ruling, and, secondly, on the need to ensure, by way of judicial review with reference to Article 19 para 1 TEU, the compliance with the conditions set out in Article 48 para 6 TEU.

Concerning the first element above, it must be stressed that the regime of Article 48 para 6 TEU does not concern a decision falling within the general decision-making process. Indeed, one should note that the European Council Decision 2011/199 is part of the high policy measures amending the Treaties for which the Treaties do not foresee any judicial review instrument at European level. In addition, after the ratification of the proposed amendment by the Member States, the new provision, as primary law, could not be subject to a review concerning its validity before the Court. The amendments of the Treaties, independently of whether they are the result of the ordinary or the simplified revision procedure, have the same legal status in the framework of the Treaties and since the establishment of the European Communities are not subject to a review before the European Union judicature.

The Court clearly decided not to take into account the fact that the European Council's Decision 2011/199 has a peculiar status and, in order to establish its jurisdiction, the Court applied *mutatis mutandis* its case law related to the validity of the EU institutions acts in the framework of a preliminary ruling procedure.

Regarding the second consideration mentioned above, it must be preliminarily observed that in the absence of an *ad hoc* mechanism provided for in the Treaties regarding the respect of the conditions laid down in Article 48 para 6 TEU, the Court implicitly considered that this review could be exercised through the general instruments provided for by the Treaties (e.g. direct actions such as action of annulment and reference for preliminary ruling).

The position of the CJEU regarding its own jurisdiction is significant because the Member States during the last Intergovernmental Conference in Lisbon did not contemplate a specific review regarding the procedural rules laid down by Article 48 para 6 TEU. By recognizing its own jurisdiction with reference to the general clause of Article 19 para 1 TEU, the CJEU clarified the physiognomy of its review, namely that the CJEU has a large jurisdiction exercised via all the judicial mechanisms and covering also the simplified revision procedure.

This reasoning of the Court is not surprising for a judicial power such as the Court. Indeed, it was impossible for the CJEU to deny its jurisdiction, even if the reference for a preliminary ruling was arguably not the appropriate mechanism to review the procedural rules laid down by Article 48 para 6 TEU. As a matter of fact, however, the circumstances under which the Court decided to establish its jurisdiction, namely the peculiar nature of the litigation before the national judge, the specific conditions of the review at national level and the fact that in any case the ESM treaty is into force have required the CJEU's to rule in a pragmatic manner.

Despite these difficulties, the CJEU recognized its jurisdiction with reference to the general clause of Article 19 para 1 TEU (former Article 220 TCE) which in the past (see Opinion Court 1/91 Draft EEA Agreement)[10] served, with some reluctances and criticisms from academia,[11] as one of the fundamental boundaries of its review. The CJEU needed a strong basis in order to justify its jurisdiction and this Article was considered as the appropriate ground.

The position of the Court needs however to be assessed in the light of the following considerations. A review of the conditions of Article 48 para 6 TEU through a reference for a preliminary ruling without limits *ratione temporis* would allow any person to challenge a decision adopted on the basis of Article 48 para 6 TFEU. The analysis of the Court concerning the admissibility of the question for the preliminary ruling on the basis that the applicant in the main proceedings could have brought a direct action under Article 263 TFEU for annulment of the Decision 2011/199 put also in evidence the peculiarity of the reasoning of the CJEU (paras 38–41).

In addition, it must be stressed that the review of the conditions of the simplified revision procedure provided for in Article 48 para 6 TEU is very close to a constitutional review which at national level is exercised in principle by constitutional courts under certain procedural conditions. Through its choice to recognize its jurisdiction in order to appreciate the validity of an act of an EU institution amending the Treaties through a preliminary ruling procedure, the Court clearly has made a choice favourable to individuals.

It should be incidentally noted that the CJEU did not make any mention of the constitutional nature of its review concerning the validity of the European Council Decision 2011/199. It is certain that given the peculiarity of its review regarding

---

[10] Opinion 1/91, of the Court, of 14 December 1991, *Draft agreement between the Community, on the one hand, and the countries of the European Free Trade Association, on the other, relating to the creation of the European Economic Area*, ECR I-6079.

[11] See, inter alia Auvret-Finck (1993), pp. 38–59 sp. 50; Boulouis (1992), pp. 457–463, sp. 462-463; Constantinesco (1992), pp. 422–426; Da Cruz Vilaça and Piçarra (1993), pp. 3–37, sp. 26; Dutheil De La Rochere (1992), pp. 603–612, sp. 610; Hartley (1992), pp. 841–848, sp. 848; Schermers (1992), pp. 991–1009, sp. 1001; Simon and Rigaux (1992), pp. 1–4.

the simplified revision procedure, the CJEU could develop without difficulties a new legal framework for a *"constitutional"* review. In the past, the CJEU made reference to the constitutional character of the Treaties[12] and consequently of its review. Nevertheless, in its last judgments, and also in the Pringle case, the Court did not use the term "constitutional" and limited itself to the general statement according to which *"the European Union is a union based on the rule of law, its institutions being subject to review of the conformity of their acts, inter alia, with the Treaty and the general principles of law"*.[13]

In the Pringle case, the position taken by the CJEU on its jurisdiction on the basis of the existing legal framework seems implicitly to take into account the specificity of the case under discussion, as well as the politically sensitive nature of the issues involved. The peculiarity of the Pringle case may justify the Court's choice to affirm its jurisdiction. However, it will be necessary to examine if in the future, and in a different—less politically sensitive—scenario, the Court will continue to exercise its control under the conditions laid down in the Pringle case or if it will choose to establish a new judicial doctrine.

2.3 Conclusion

The CJEU recognized firstly its jurisdiction to interpret an international agreement concluded exclusively by Member States and, secondly, its jurisdiction regarding the validity of an EU institution's act amending the Treaties under the conditions laid down by Article 48 para 6 TEU. In both cases, the Court developed its reasoning in line with its previous case law, which was elaborated in a context different than the peculiar framework of a simplified revision procedure.

Concerning the jurisdiction of the Court to interpret international agreements concluded exclusively by the Member States, one could argue prima facie that the CJEU deviates from its previous case law. Such agreements do not fall within the Court jurisdiction and in that respect the Court did not wish to establish an exception to its previous case law. It is certain that the Court had to develop a very specific reasoning and that in particular when, on the basis of its case law, it was easy to declare that the Court had not jurisdiction.

The Court preferred to ground its jurisdiction on the necessity to ensure a uniform interpretation by all the national judges and used its well known statement according to which the Court has *"to give the national court full guidance on the interpretation of European Union law in order to enable it to determine the issue of compatibility of a national measure with that law for the purposes of deciding the case before it"*. This statement of the Court must be welcomed because firstly it enlarges the jurisdiction on the basis of the Court's own judicial power

[12] Case 294/83, *"Les Verts" v European Parliament*, [1986] ECR 1339, para 23.

[13] Case C-336/09 P, *Republic of Poland v European Commission*, [2012], Judgment of the Court of 26 June 2012, nyr, para 36 and the cited case-law.

and secondly because the Court reminds the national courts that it has the exclusive privilege as the authentic interpreter of the primary provisions of European law. This position of the Court could be also considered as the answer of the European Union judicature to the national court when the latter avails itself of the well known doctrine of *"acte clair"*.

It is true that as the highest judicial authority of the European Union, the Court could elaborate this reasoning without adhering strictly to its previous case law but it come as no surprise that the Court refers to past decisions to corroborate its reasoning. On the basis of the Pringle judgment, in the future, an agreement concluded exclusively by the Member States, as for instance the STACOG Treaty or the EFSF Framework Agreement, could be subject to the control of the Court in the framework of a reference for a preliminary ruling.

Concerning the jurisdiction of the Court regarding the validity of a European Council Decision 2011/199 amending a primary law provision under the conditions of Article 48 para 6 TEU, the Court decided to consider that this decision adopted on the basis of Article 48 para 6 TEU was an act of an EU institution for which, in any case, the Court has jurisdiction. However, one could argue that the Court even in that context has no jurisdiction to interpret amendments to the treaties.[14] Indeed, regardless of the fact that a European Council Decision is a EU act *rationae materiae*, it concerns an amendment of a EU primary law.

There is certainly a difference between the ordinary revision procedure on the basis of which the Court established initially its case law and the particular context of the simplified revision procedure which is the subject of the Court review. It is certain that a European Council Decision 2011/199 adopted on the basis of Article 48 para 6 TEU may not be assimilated ipso facto to an act of a European institution elaborated in the framework of the EU decision making process. The Court appears to consider this peculiarity and, faced with the sensitivity of the question, decided to justify its jurisdiction by reference to Article 19 TEU which is the general clause justifying the Court's activism. This position of the Court was also necessary as the Treaties did not provide any specific review mechanism concerning the simplified revision procedure.

The above mentioned statement of the Court has other consequences. Based on the Pringle judgment, it could not be excluded that individuals could activate a review of a European Council Decision adopted in the framework of the simplified revision procedure by initiating a proceeding before the Court via the preliminary ruling mechanism. The reasoning developed by the Court regarding the admissibility of the question of the referring judge confirms this perspective. Given the peculiarity of the context of the review of the Court, it remains to be seen whether the Court will continue to review similar cases in the light of the Pringle judgment, or if the Member States will decide to revise the Treaties and establish an *ad hoc* procedure at primary law level. In this respect, it could be envisaged for instance the establishment of a preventive review comparable to the procedure for

[14] Case C-253/94 P, *Roujansky v Council of the European Union*, Order of 13 January 1995, ECR I-7. See in that respect Van Malleghem (2013), pp. 141–168, sp. 156.

an opinion such provided in the field of the EU external relations in Article 218 para 11 TFEU. This perspective could be envisaged in the next formal revision of the Treaties.

References

Auvret-Finck J (1993) Les avis 1-91 et 1-92 relatifs au projet d'accord sur la création de l'espace économique européen. CDE:38–59

Boulouis J (1992) Les avis de la Cour de justice des Communautés sur la compatibilité avec le Traité CEE du projet d'accord créant l'Espace économique européen. RTDE:457–463

Constantinesco V (1992) Commentaire de l'avis 1/91, Chronique de jurisprudence de la Cour de justice des Communautés européennes. Institutions et ordre juridique Communautaire. JDI (Clunet):422–426

Da Cruz Vilaça JL, Piçarra N (1993) Y a-t-il des limites matérielles à la révision des traités instituant les communautés européennes? CDE:3–37

Dechatre L (2011) La décision de Karlsruhe sur le mécanisme de stabilité financière: une validité sous conditions et une mise en garde sibylline pour l'avenir. CDE:303–342

Dutheil De La Rochere J (1992) L'espace économique européen sous le regard des juges de la Cour de justice des Communautés européennes. RMC:603–612

Hartley T (1992) The European court and the EEA. ICLQ:841–848

Partsch PE, Robberecht E (2013) Chronique: Recent case law and decisions in European banking and financial law (September 2011–Decmber 2012). CFCMLR/RTDF:77

Schermers HG (1992) Comments on opinion 1/91. CMLRev:991–1009

Schmidt SK (2013) A sense of Déjà Vu? The FCC's Preliminary European Stability Verdict. GLJ:1–19

Simon D, Rigaux A (1992) L'avis de la Cour de justice sur le projet d'accord CEE/AELE portant création de l'Espace économique européen (EEE). Europe :1–4

Van Malleghem P-A (2013) Pringle: a paradigm shift in the European Union's monetary constitution. GLJ:141–168

Chapter 3
The Simplified Revision Procedure of Article 48 para 6 TEU and the Possible Amendments of the EMU Framework

The Court developed a specific approach concerning the simplified revision procedure, such as provided for the first time in the European Treaties in Article 48 para 6 TEU. In the absence of a specific procedure concerning this review, the Court laid out the general framework under which its review must be carried out in the context of a reference for a preliminary ruling.

The Court examined, firstly, if the European Council Decision 2011/199 concerns exclusively part III of the TFEU (Article 48 para 6 TEU first and second subparagraphs). In this respect the Court developed a dynamic reasoning. It did not limit its review to the formal requirements of this provision, but also examined the substantive requirement implicitly contained in this provision. The Court developed a new reasoning according to which the proposed amendment under Article 48 para 6 TEU must not affect other parts of the TFEU. In this context, the Court developed a new concept: that of the "*safeguard of the stability of the euro area as a whole*", which is the concept on which the whole reasoning of the Court revolves (**3.1**).

Secondly, the Court examined if the proposed modification increases the competences conferred on the Union in the Treaties (Article 48 para 6 TEU third subparagraph) (**3.2**). In that part of the judgment, the Court did not have particular problems to demonstrate that the conditions not to increase the competences conferred on the Union are fulfilled.

3.1 Amendments of Part III of the TFEU

Article 48 para 6 TEU provides that the simplified revision procedure applies to the provisions of part III of the TFEU. In relation to this formal requirement (**3.1.1**), the Pringle judgment states that the simplified revision procedure cannot be used to circumvent the ordinary revision procedure under which it is possible to amend in substance part I (or part II) of the TFEU (**3.2.2**). In this context, the

E. de Lhoneux and C. A. Vassilopoulos, *The European Stability Mechanism Before the Court of Justice of the European Union*, SpringerBriefs in Law,
DOI: 10.1007/978-3-319-01478-4_3, © The Author(s) 2014

Court developed a specific reasoning according to which the amendment proposed under Article 48 para 6 TEU must not affect other parts of the TFEU.

3.1.1 The formal requirements

Concerning the formal condition mentioned above, the CJEU observed that the European Council Decision 2011/199 amends a provision of part III of the TFEU (Article 136) and thereby formally *"satisfies the condition stated in the first and second subparagraphs of Article 48 para 6 TEU"* (para 46). It can be inferred from the above that any provision on the Economic and Monetary policies (Articles 119 TFEU to 144 TFEU), which are formally contained in part III of the TFEU could, as such, be subject to an amendment proposal pursuant to the simplified revision procedure.

Given the reference to *"part III of the TFEU"* in Article 48 para 6 TEU, and the position of the Court concerning Article 136 TFEU, it is interesting to examine whether the other provisions of the Treaty concerning the EMU, such as the provisions of the Protocol on the Statute of the European System of Central banks (ESCB) and of the European Central Bank (ECB) (Protocol 4), could be subject to amendments on the basis of this Article.

A formal reading of Article 48 para 6 TEU seems to rule out such a possibility, as formally Protocol 4 is not a part of the TFEU. However, given the similarity of many provisions in Protocol 4 with title VII of part III of the TFEU, the application of the simplified revision procedure to the Protocol cannot be excluded *tout-court*. In addition to Article 51 TEU, which provides that protocols and annexes to the treaties *"shall form an integral part thereof"*, it must be underlined that Article 129 para 2 TFEU, that is to say a provision of part III of the TFEU, refers to the statute of the ESCB and the ECB. These elements might support the conclusion that the provisions of Protocol 4 could also be subject to the procedure set out in Article 48 para 6 TEU.

It results from the above that according to Article 48 para 6 TEU and the interpretation given by the CJEU of the formal requirements of this Article, the regime of the monetary and economic pillars of the EMU, including Protocol 4, could in principle be amended on the basis of a simplified revision procedure.

Concerning in particular the monetary policy, as it will be analyzed further in this study, one could observe that this is an exclusive competence of the EU which, as such, cannot be subject to amendments by Member States acting in the framework of Article 48 para 6 TEU but rather in the framework of the ordinary revision procedure, and that in order not to modify the balance and play of competences such as provided for in the Treaties. However, it is important to observe that formally the authors of the Treaties did not exclude *tout-court* the monetary pillar of the EMU from the simplified revision procedure. It seems therefore that for the authors of the Treaties some elements not falling within the hard core provisions of the monetary policy and the monetary pillar could be amended via the simplified revision procedure.

For instance, the prudential supervision of credit institutions is not part of the hard provisions of monetary policy.[1] The authors of the Treaties provided in Article 127 para 6 TFEU—that is to say a provision of part III of the TFEU and the first monetary policy provision of Chap. 2 of title VII of part III—for the possibility to confer on the ECB the prudential supervision of credit institutions and other financial institutions. One could therefore argue that the simplified revision procedure could be applicable in this framework and probably this could be one of the reasons why the authors of the Treaties did not limit the scope of the simplified revision procedure in the Chap. 2 of the Title VII part III of the TFEU.

Furthermore, bearing in mind these considerations and following the request of the referring court, the CJEU examined whether the formal revision of provisions of part III of the TFEU could affect also the provisions of part I of the TFEU.

3.1.2 The substantial requirements: amendments not affecting other parts of the TFEU

The CJEU developed a two-prong reasoning in order to establish that the proposed amendment of Article 136 TFEU by European Council Decision 2011/199 is in line with the Treaties. The Court concluded that this amendment does not infringe the rules governing the EU exclusive competence in the field of the monetary policy (**3.1.2.1**) nor the regime provided for in the Treaties regarding the coordination of the economic policies of the Member States **(3.1.2.2).**

3.1.2.1 Non infringement of the rules governing the EU exclusive competence

If the proposed amendment of Article 136 TFEU—part III of the TFEU—is considered as falling within monetary policy, this amendment could possibly modify the content or the scope of this policy which, according to Article 3 para 1c TFEU—provision of part I of the TFEU—is an exclusive competence of the EU.[2] Therefore, even if the first condition laid down by Article 48 para 6 TEU was formally respected, it could be argued that the proposed amendment of Article 136

[1] In the proposal for a regulation conferring specific tasks on the ECB concerning policies relating to the prudential supervision for credit institution, which will be adopted by the Council on the basis of Article 127 para 6 TFEU, it is formally provided for (Article 25 para 2—*Separation from Monetary Policy function*) that *"(th)e ECB shall carry out the tasks conferred upon it by this Regulation without prejudice to and separately from its tasks relating to the monetary policy and the other tasks".*

[2] It must be reminded that when the Treaties confer on the Union an exclusive competence in a specific area such as the monetary policy according to Article 2 para 1 TFEU, only the EU institutions may legislate and adopt legally binding acts, the Member States being able to do so themselves only if so empowered by the Union or for the implementation of the European Union acts.

TFEU infringes the provisions of another part of the TFEU. This is, in substance, one of the questions referred by the national judge.

The CJEU reminded, on the one hand, the Articles of the Treaties conferring an exclusive competence on the EU in the field of monetary policy and stressed that the conduct of this policy is managed within an independent institutional framework (paras 48–50). On the other hand, the Court observed that the TFEU does not define "monetary policy" but it refers to *"the objectives rather that to instruments of the monetary policy"* (para 53).

As a preliminary comment on the position of the CJEU regarding the absence of a definition concerning monetary policy, it must be observed that the Court developed a reasoning in line with its case-law on other common policies of the EU. As a matter of fact, since the establishment of the European Communities, the European Treaties did not contain any definition of several European (Community) policies. It has been the task of the Court, along the years, to gradually determine, in its case-law, the physiognomy and content of these policies (trade policy, environment policy, social policy etc.). It is in fact in these matters that the Court developed the first steps of its case law showing a vision about its own role in the elaboration of EU law.

While the application of such method appears justified in relation to other common policies, in the field of monetary policy the situation appears rather different. It is difficult to conceive that the European Treaties, that is to say formal international acts with their *sui generis* characteristics, could contain a definition of monetary policy and in the absence of such a definition the Court, that is to say a judicial institution, could, similarly to the other common EU policies, determine its content and scope. Even at national level and before the introduction of the euro, no constitution in Western Europe did provide for an exact and detailed content of monetary policy, and it could not be envisaged that a judicial power could intervene to fill such gap. The reason for this is that the definition of the scope of this policy depends on technical and economic considerations and standards as well as a degree of discretion which can typically be found at a sovereign level and, therefore, normally falls outside of the expertise of a traditional judicial power.

In that respect, it must be reminded that also the Court admitted to exercise a restraint review relating to the decisions adopted in the field of economic law, when it was necessary to formulate economic considerations in areas such as competition, antidumping etc. For that reason, the judicial control has been limited to some procedural aspects without interfering in the definition of the content of these policies which still remain within the discretionary power of the relevant competent authorities.

Despite its tradition in this matter, the Court preferred to take a clear position about the field of monetary policy and to develop some considerations with important legal and economic implications. The Court therefore inaugurated a rather new approach on the technicality and the specificity of the issue concerning a high level policy such as monetary policy. In that respect, and in order to justify that the amendment of Article 136 TFEU does not encroach upon the rules governing the exclusive competence of the EU, the Court developed a three steps reasoning.

Firstly, the Court states that the primary objective of the European Union's monetary policy is to maintain price stability (para 54), and that the objective pursued by the envisaged stability mechanism provided for by the European Council Decision 2011/199 is to safeguard *"the stability of the euro area as a whole"*, which *"is clearly distinct from the objective of maintaining price stability which is the primary objective of the European Union's monetary policy"* (para 56).

In para 56, the Court uses the terms *"the stability of the euro area"* and not the term *"financial"* stability or the *"stability of the financial system"*. It seems that the Court draws this expression from Article 12 para 1 of the ESM Treaty which expressly mentions the goal to *"safeguard the financial stability of the euro area as a whole"* and directly also from the European Council Decision 2011/199 (proposed amendment of Article 136 TFEU). The only difference between, on the one hand, the text of Article 12 para 1 and European Council Decision 2011/199 and, on the other hand, the wording used by the Court in para 56 is that in the latter the word *"financial"* has been omitted. In this respect, one could argue that the Court considered that the stability of the euro area and the financial stability of the euro area as a whole are equivalent concepts. In any case, one should note that the Court draws inspiration from an international treaty between Member States, which is subject to its judicial review, rather than from one or more provisions of the European Union treaties.

The CJEU innovates with the concept of the *"stability of the euro area as a whole"* as an objective which is a separate concept from price stability and found in this new concept the justification according to which the new stability mechanism does not concern monetary policy. In the same perspective, one could argue that as an autonomous concept, the safeguard of the stability of the euro area as a whole could imply a sort of obligation for Member States to provide financial assistance and/or increasing the financial capacity of the ESM. Further, it could be also envisaged that the concept of stability of the euro area implies the preservation of the integrity of the euro area and therefore the obligation for the (euro area) Member States to adopt all the necessary measures to avoid the exit of one of such Members of the euro area.

While the innovative character of the Court's reasoning should be appreciated, one could observe that price stability and stability of the euro area as objectives have complementary functions. Indeed, it could not be excluded that price stability contributes to the stability of the euro area and, in any case, on a more general level, there appears to be an interaction between the two concepts.

The reasoning of the CJEU presents an additional interesting element in the second sentence of the same para 56. According to this sentence, *"even though the stability of the euro area may have repercussions on the stability of the currencies used within that area, an economic policy measure cannot be treated as equivalent to a monetary policy measure for the sole reason that it may have a direct effect on the stability of the euro"*.

On the basis of this statement, one could argue that an economic policy measure can be treated as *equivalent* to a monetary policy measure. One could ask the question of what the Court considered exactly as an economic measure **equivalent** to a monetary policy measure. It would require a very careful appreciation for a judicial authority to determine whether or not a measure is part of monetary policy, also in the light of the fact that never in the past a judge has in principle exercised such assessment in the field of his powers.

The position of the CJEU on this point constitutes a new element which signals that the Court might increasingly participate via its case law to the elaboration of the EMU framework. In any case, the Court draws the concept of safeguard of the stability of the euro area as whole in order to justify that the modification in Article 136 TFEU does not encroach upon the monetary policy whose objective remains price stability. For the Court, the safeguard of the stability of the euro area as a whole justifies in fact the establishment of a stability mechanism such as the ESM Treaty.

In order to strengthen the first step of its reasoning, the CJEU, secondly, confirms that the objective of *"the stability of the euro area"* is completely independent from the monetary policy as for its instruments. In this regard, the CJEU stressed that European Council Decision 2011/199 provides that the stability mechanism will grant any required financial assistance and, in the absence of any other information on the operation of this mechanism, the CJEU concluded that *"the grant of financial assistance to a member state, however, clearly does not fall within monetary policy"* (para 57).

There is no doubt that the financial assistance to a Member State of the EU is not to be considered as a monetary policy measure. On the basis of this element, the CJEU could take its position without further consideration regarding the scope and the objectives of the monetary policy in relation to the financial stability or the stability of the euro area.

Continuing its reasoning and in order to further reinforce its position, the Court observed thirdly that the stability mechanism serves to complement the new regulatory framework for strengthening the economic governance of the European Union. The Court concluded that, in addition to Articles 123 TFEU and 125 TFEU and the Stability and Growth Pact, as amended in 2011, which have essentially a preventive function in order to reduce the risk of public debt crisis, the objective of the stability mechanism *"is the management of the financial crisis"* (paras 58–59) even when the preventive measures fail their objective.

In the above mentioned paragraphs, the Court recognized that the envisaged modifications to Article 136 TFEU complete the legal instruments adopted concerning the economic pillar of the EMU, in particular the SGP framework. There is not doubt that these instruments do not concern per se the monetary policy, it was therefore logical for the Court to conclude that the envisaged amendment of Article 136 TFEU is not able to affect the exclusive competence of the EU in the filed of the monetary policy. However, the intermediate conclusion of the Court is that the establishment of the stability mechanism falls within the field of the economic policy (para 60)!

In addition, a comment must be made in relation to the position of the Court regarding the impact of the consultation of the ECB on the modification concerning Article 136 TFEU. In that respect, it was argued before the Court that the consultation of the ECB in the framework of the procedure of Article 48 para 6 TEU constitutes in fact evidence that the stability mechanism is related to the monetary policy. As a response, the CJEU stressed that it "*is clearly apparent from the wording of recital 5*" of the preamble of the European Council Decision 2011/199 that the European Council consulted the ECB on its own initiative and not because it was under an obligation under the treaty (para 61).

The CJEU justified its position on the basis of the consideration that the consultation of the ECB under the framework of Article 48 para 6 TEU is the result of the initiative of the European Council. Indeed, it results clearly from the above mentioned decision that the European Council decided to consult the ECB. Nevertheless, as results from the same recital 5 of the same decision, the European Council decided in addition to consult the European Parliament and the Commission on the relevant proposal. Nobody could maintain that these EU institutions delivered their opinions exclusively because the European Council invited them to participate to the simplified revision procedure. In addition, it must be observed that in recital 5 of the preamble of the European Council Decision 2011/199 the same words are used for all the institutions involved.

For avoidance of doubts, the CJEU added that "*in any event, the consultation of the ECB on the draft decision 2011/199 cannot affect the nature of the envisaged stability mechanism...*" (para 62).

It is certain that, with this paragraph, the CJEU made an effort to demonstrate that the consultation of the ECB in the framework of the simplified revision procedure could not be considered as evidence that the European Council Decision 2011/199 falls into the monetary policy field. The Court opted for a complex formulation: the CJEU referred to the "*nature of...the stability mechanism*" although the issue in the case was whether the stability mechanism fell or not within the area of monetary policy.

It results from the above that the Court used an articulated reasoning in order to demonstrate that the modifications in Article 136 TFEU do not encroach upon the monetary policy which is an exclusive competence of the EU. This reasoning is largely convincing. The Court made important efforts to structure legally an economic reasoning, and proceeded very close to technical and complex assessments which are generally left outside the scope of the judicial review. The main reason for this "*judicial behaviour*" is in fact that the Court is the supreme jurisdiction at European level. It is not certain if the same assessments made for instance by the General Court in relation to the objective to safeguard the stability of the euro area or to the existence of economic measures equivalent to a monetary policy measures will be accepted in case of an appeal before the Court.

Furthermore, the Court needed also to justify that the envisaged stability mechanism does not alter the EU rules regarding the coordination of the economic policy of the Member States. This issue is discussed below.

3.1.2.2 No alteration of the EU rules

A further question the Court had to address was whether a stability mechanism, such as that envisaged by the European Council Decision 2011/199 amending

Article 136 TFEU, affects the competence of the Union in the area of the coordination of the Member States' economic policy as determined in the part I of the TFEU.

In contrast to the monetary policy, in the economic field, the amendments of part III of the TFEU are not capable of infringing in principle the fundamental rules provided for by the treaties in Part I TFEU. This is because in this field the treaties do not confer an exclusive competence to the EU. The peculiarity of the economic policy is that the Treaties do not qualify the EU competence in this area as "shared", rather they contain specific provisions i.e. Articles 2 para 3 TFEU and Article 5 para 1 TFEU from which it results that the EU has a peculiar role.

The Court observed that given the fact that Articles 2 para 3 and 5 para 1 TFEU restrict the role of the EU in the area of economic policy to the adoption of coordinating measures, the Treaties do not confer any specific power on the Union to establish a stability mechanism such as that envisaged by the European Council Decision 2011/199 (para 64). The Court emphasized that the main role of the EU institutions is limited to the coordination of the national actions and not the adoption of rules *ratione materiae* in order to put in place a gradual harmonization of the economic policies of the Member States. Indeed, the limited role of the European Institutions to develop rules in order to coordinate the action of the Member States in that field does not affect the privilege of the Member States to develop and to determine the substance of their economic policies.

However, given that Articles 122 para 2 TFEU and 143 para 2 TFEU confer on the EU institutions a particular power to act in relation to the economic policies, the Court had to take position and that in particular on the basis of a full argumentation developed before the CJEU. In addition, the Court developed a specific reasoning regarding the non application of Article 352 TFEU according to which the Treaties confer on the Council the power to act if an action by the Union should prove necessary within the framework of the policies defined in the Treaties. Indeed, the use of this provision could be the basis to establish a financial stability mechanism.

Concerning firstly Article 122 para 2 TFEU, this provision recognizes that the Council can grant financial assistance to a Member State when this State is in difficulties or is seriously threatened with severe difficulties caused by natural disasters or exceptional occurrences beyond its control. According to the Court, this Article confers a specific competence in the field of financial assistance on the Union. Nevertheless it does not constitute an appropriate legal basis for the establishment of a stability mechanism such as that envisaged by the European Council Decision 2011/199 as such mechanism *"is to be permanent and its objectives are to safeguard the financial stability of the euro area as whole"* (para 65).

In para 65, the CJEU pointed out two main elements/justifications allowing to amend Article 136 TFEU without infringing Articles 122 para 2 TFEU. The first concerns the permanent character of the stability mechanism envisaged by the proposed amendment. The second is in relation to the concept mentioned in para 56 of the Pringle judgment that is to say the preservation *"of the stability of the euro area as whole."*

Regarding the first justification above, for the CJEU this new stability mechanism has a permanent character whereas Article 122 para 2 TFEU concerns temporary measures. The distinction between the temporary and permanent nature of the financial assistance used by the CJEU to support that Article 122 para 2 TFEU is not applicable in order to adopt EU financial assistance measures such as the stability mechanism.

The Court followed a prudent approach and preferred not to develop any argumentation supported before national jurisdictions according to which the EU measures adopted on the basis of Article 122 TFEU are conditional upon the existence of difficulties or natural disasters or exceptional occurrences whereas the envisaged stability mechanism is not conditional upon those elements. In addition, the Court did not put in evidence that the assistance granted on the basis of Article 122 para 2 TFEU finds its economic source in the European budget, whereas the stability mechanism provides a direct financial assistance from the Member States. In the same vein, the Court did not develop a reasoning according to which Article 122 para 2 TFEU applies where there is an impossibility for a Member State to meet its financial obligations. Clarifications in the statement of the Court inspired from these arguments could have helped define the difference between the regimes of Article 122 para 2 TFEU and of the ESM Treaty. However, the Court decided to stay silent in this matter.

Regarding the second justification, for the CJEU the financial assistance put in place by the envisaged stability mechanism aims to safeguard *"the stability of the euro area as whole"* and it seems that this is not the objective of the measures adopted in the framework of Article 122 para 2 TFEU which had in fact a restricted scope. The new jurisprudential concept of *"the stability of the euro area as whole"* is for the Court the main basis to justify its statement in the field of the financial assistance contemplated by the stability mechanism.

Concerning secondly Article 143 para 2 TFEU, the CJEU reminded that under certain conditions this provision enables the EU to grant mutual assistance to the Member States but considers that this possibility concerns exclusively Member States whose currency is not the Euro (para 66). In that respect, on the basis of this Article, the European Union granted mutual assistance for some non-euro area Member States (Romania, Latvia, Hungary).[3]

The CJEU recognizes in fact that Article 143 para 2 TFEU provides for the possibility to grant assistance only outside the euro area which is not the case for the stability mechanism which is applicable to Member States whose currency is the euro. Assuming, as suggested by the CJEU, that Article 143 para 2 TFEU contains a safeguard provision only for the Member States outside the euro zone, would mean that the treaties allow only to provide financial assistance for Member States which are not part of the euro area and not for euro area Member States! Formally

[3] Council Decision n°2009/103/EC of 4 November 2008 granting mutual assistance for Hungary (OJ L 37, p. 7) ; Council Decision n°2009/289/EC of 20 January 2009 granting mutual assistance for Latvia (OJ L 79, p. 37); Council Decision n°2009/458/EC of 6 May 2009 granting mutual assistance for Romania (OJ L 150, p. 6).

this reasoning is correct. For someone,[4] this situation is logical since, given the regime of the EMU, it is not envisaged to adopt a financial mechanism for the euro zone Member States. This position should however be nuanced.

It is certain that the regime applicable to the EMU could not be compared to the regime provided by the European Treaties for non euro Member States. However, the financial assistance domain is part of the economic pillar of the EMU and, as also recognized by the Pringle judgment, in the field of economic policy, the European Union, contrary to monetary policy, has not an exclusive competence. In this context, an intervention of the EU institutions must not be de facto excluded. It does not seem coherent to provide a financial stability mechanism for Member States outside the euro zone and not for the euro area Member States when the economic policy still remains within Member State competence. Prudently, the Court avoided to further develop its reasoning in that respect, as probably such reasoning in relation to the regime of Article 122 para 2 TFEU would risk to create confusion about the perimeter of the EU competence as determined in the Treaties.

In the light of the regime set out in Articles 122 para 2 TFEU and 143 para 2 TFEU one could argue that, alternatively to the interpretative route chosen by the Court, the Treaties do in fact contain material rules governing the EU competence on financial assistance and therefore do not limit this competence to the adoption of coordination rules. This point is not addressed in the judgment.

The position of the Court becomes more interesting when the Court developed thirdly an argumentation concerning the non application of Article 352 TFEU in para 67 of the judgment. Probably responding to an argument raised during the proceeding—the Court stated that the EU could not establish the proposed stability mechanism on the basis of Article 352 TFEU (former 308 TEC), because the Union had not used its powers under this Article and, in any case, this provision does not impose on the Union any obligation to act. The Court made reference to the well-known ERTA[5] case.

In its judgment, the Court did not develop an in-depth reasoning regarding the possibility to use or not Article 352 TFEU as a legal basis for granting the EU institutions competence regarding the financial assistance to Member States. It must be reminded that the relevant criterion for the application of Article 352 TFEU is the necessity to act. This provision refers to an action which *"should prove necessary"* when the Treaties had *"not provided for the necessary powers"*. One could argue that this condition was in fact existent in the present instance as there was a real necessity to adopt a stability mechanism to tackle the financial crisis. In addition, one could maintain that the use of Article 352 TFEU was necessary and desirable given the fact that Article 122 para 2 TFEU and Article 143 para 2 TFEU provide for some ad hoc EU measures and not for a full stability mechanism.

---

[4] See Allemand and Martucci (2012), pp. 409–457, sp. 412–413.

[5] Case 22/70, *Commission v Council (ERTA)*, [1971] ECR 263.

The Court stated its position with an obiter dictum according to which Article 352 TFEU does not impose any obligation to act on the EU. However, the absence of any obligation to act does not eliminate *per se* the competence of the relevant EU institution in this field.

The CJEU might have wanted to point out that for the moment the EU did not exercise its competence in the financial assistance field and in that respect the Member States could exercise such competence in the absence of concrete EU measures. It is evident that, in the absence of any EU measure, the question of the alteration of the EU competence becomes irrelevant. Therefore, the Court stated that there was no alteration of the EU rules regarding the coordination of economic policies as provided in the Treaties.

Under those conditions, the Court concluded that Member States whose currency is the euro are entitled to enter into an agreement between themselves for the establishment of a stability mechanism as envisaged by the European Council Decision 2011/199. However, according to the Court, those Member States may not disregard their duty to comply with European Union law when exercising their competence in that area. In addition, the Court also considered that the *"conditionality"* of the financial assistance, such as *expessis verbis* provided for in the new Article 136 para 3 TFEU, is provided for in order to ensure that the stability mechanism will operate in a way that will comply with European Union law, including the measures adopted by the EU in the context of the coordination of the Member States' economic policies (paras 68–69).

The Court's reasoning is quasi-identical to the case law[6] on the rules regarding the conclusion of international agreements in the absence of any express provision in the Treaties. In particular, the CJEU referred to its case law in the field of development (in particular, the field of humanitarian and development aid).[7] The CJEU referred to this case law even if the rules elaborated by the Court in the field of EU external relations (exercise and nature of competences) might not be considered as applicable *ipso facto* to the regime of the unilateral actions of the Member States which is relevant for the Pringle case.

Probably aware of such aspect, the Court pointed out, with reference to the Gottardo case, that the Member States may not disregard their duty to comply with European Union law when exercising their competences in the area of the economic policy. In this case, concerning a bilateral double taxation treaty concluded between a Member State and a non-member country, the Court concluded that, although direct taxation is a matter falling within the competence of the Member States alone, the latter may not disregard Community rules and must exercise their

---

[6] See, for instance, Opinion 1/03, *Competence of the Community to conclude the new Lugano Convention on jurisdiction and the recognition and enforcement of judgments in civil and commercial matters*, [2006] ECR I-1145, paras 114 and f.

[7] See Joined cases C-181/91 and C-248/91, *European Parliament v Council and Commission*, [1993] ECR I-3685 (humanitarian aid) and Case C-316/91, *European Parliament v Council*, [1994] ECR I-625 (development aid).

powers in a manner consistent with Community law.[8] For the CJEU this reasoning could be perfectly applicable in the case at glance even if the field of direct taxation does not present exactly the same issues regarding the financial assistance of the Member States.

The reasoning of the Court applied by analogy in the present case and largely inspired by its case law in the area of development has the peculiarity to be based on the rules elaborated in the framework of the Maastricht treaty. In that context, the rules concerning the nature of the exercise of EU competence had mainly jurisprudential origin and, unlike today, did not enjoy primary law status. The CJEU constructed its global reasoning on the basis of this previous case law although the context of the Pringle litigation, that is to say the simplified revision procedure, and the *ratione materiae* issues i.e. the EMU, were totally new subjects for the European jurisprudence. This approach characterizes the Pringle judgment as a whole. The Court preferred to quote and apply by analogy its case law rather than to innovate and create a completely new stream of case law.

However, it cannot be said that the Court did not make any effort to construct a new jurisprudence and that for two reasons.

Firstly, the CJEU considered that there is a new objective, the preservation *"of the stability of the euro area as whole"*, which must be taken into account in order to determine the scope of the envisaged financial assistance regime. In practice, this new objective allowed the CJEU to conclude that the proposed amendment to the new Article 136 para 3 TFEU did not concern monetary policy and, in any case, goes beyond the specific objectives of some articles conferring a competence in the EU institutions in the economic area. The intention of the Court to confer to the objective of the preservation of the stability of the euro area a large scope could have other consequences, for instance one could argue that that this aim can be applicable also to the monetary pillar of the EMU and in general the institutional framework of the ESCB. The future will tell whether this will be the case or not.

Secondly, the CJEU pointed out that the *"conditionality"* of the financial assistance aims to ensure that the stability mechanism will operate in a way that complies with European Union law, including the measures adopted by the EU in the context of the coordination of Member States' economic policies. This is to be welcomed as it clarifies the content of the amendment proposed in Article 136 para 3 TFEU. For the CJEU the *"conditionality"* of the assistance is the evidence of the peculiar nature of Member States' competence in the field of economic affairs. In many parts of the Pringle judgment, the Court makes reference to the conditionality principle with the aim of strengthening its reasoning regarding the nature of the competence in the field of financial assistance.

[8] Case C-55/00, *Elide Gottardo*, [2002] ECR I-413.

3.2 The Condition not to Increase the Competences Conferred on the Union

The CJEU had also to examine the second condition laid down in Article 48 para 6 TEU that is to say whether the European Council Decision 2011/199 amending Article 136 TFEU increases the competences conferred on the European Union in the Treaties.

The Court stated that Article 136 para 3 TFEU, as inserted by European Council Decision 2011/199, ***"confirms"*** that Member States have the power to establish the stability mechanism and is further intended to ensure that the mechanism will operate in a way that is compliant with EU law, by providing that the granting of any financial assistance under that mechanism will be made subject to strict conditionality (para 72).

It is interesting that the CJEU used the term *"confirms"* in order to declare that Member States could act unilaterally in order to establish a stability mechanism. For the Court, it follows from the amendment of Article 136 para 3 TFEU that in the field of financial assistance the Member States have the "main" competence to act. In this respect, the wording of the proposed amendment is unambiguous. Indeed, Article 136 para 3 TFEU confers the competence on the Member States, and not on the Council. In this context, the Court pointed out that this amendment does not create a legal basis for the Union to undertake any action in the area of financial assistance (para 73).

It results clearly from the reasoning of the Court that the proposed amendment of Article 136 TFEU does not constitute a legal basis for a possible action of the EU institutions in order to establish a stability mechanism. For the Court there is no question that the new provision increases a competence conferred to the European Union in the Treaties, because the provision added to Article 136 TFEU did not confer any competence upon the European Union.

Independently of this conclusion, the Court had to answer to an argumentation developed during the written procedure and the hearing according to which the participation of the EU institutions in the ESM framework is evidence that the amendment to Article 136 TFEU confers a new competence on the European Union in the field of financial assistance.

In that respect, the CJEU stated that *"even though the ESM Treaty makes use of the Union institutions* (Commission, ECB), *this is not in any event capable of affecting the validity of European Council Decision 2011/199, which in itself only provides for the establishment of a stability mechanism by the member states and is silent on any possible role for the European Union institutions in that connection"* (para 74). On this paragraph, the following comments appear necessary.

Firstly, the silence in the European Council Decision 2011/199 about any possible role of the EU institutions is justified because this decision confirms that Member States have the power to establish the stability mechanism and not the EU. In that respect, the position of the Court put in evidence the context of the adoption of the new stability mechanism outside the EU framework.

Secondly, it is interesting to observe that the Court developed its reasoning in relation to the ESM Treaty according to which this Treaty establishes a role for European Union institutions in its framework and concludes that this role is not capable of affecting the validity of the European Council Decision 2011. One could say that it was not necessary for the Court to establish a link between the ESM Treaty and the European Council Decision in order to justify that the validity of the European Council decision is not affected by the involvement of EU institutions. The issue regarding the use of the EU institutions in the ESM Treaty is independent from the question to know whether the conditions laid down by Article 48 para 6 TEU are fully respected. This is perhaps a part of the judgment that could have been further developed.

3.3 Conclusion

In the Pringle case, the CJEU examined for the first time the conditions laid down by Article 48 para 6 TEU on the simplified procedure for the revision of the Treaties. Leaving aside the issues on the exercise of such control in the context of a reference for a preliminary ruling, it should be noted that the Court clarified the content of such conditions.

Indeed, while the Article 48 para 6 TEU only refers to part III of the TFEU, the Court considered that a formal amendment of the provisions of part III TFEU must not encroach upon the other parts of the treaty, notably part I and II. In other words, the Court considered that the simplified revision procedure is not a tool to circumvent the ordinary revision procedure, which is applicable to all the parts of the TFEU and the Protocols. This is one of the most important lessons of the Pringle judgment. The conditions of the revision of the Treaties has been often subject to criticisms because the provided revision process attests in large part the degree of "constitutionalisation" of the European Treaties.[9] In that regard, the Court courageously put in perspective this reading of the conditions laid down by Article 48 para 6 TEU and, by doing so, reminded that the European Union judicature continues to have an important role in the elaboration of European Law.

It must be also observed that the Court in the Pringle judgment admits the possibility to use the simplified revision procedure in order to complement the framework of the economic pillar of the EMU. This is a highly important element, in the light of the developments concerning the Banking Union. For instance, the simplified revision procedure could be used by the Member States in order to adjust the legal framework of the prudential supervision and resolution.

In addition to the formal conditions concerning the application of Article 48 para 6 TEU, this part of the judgment allowed the Court to develop a new and

---

[9] See inter alia Quesada (2013), The revision Procedures of the Treaty, pp. 323–342, sp. 333; see also Lenaerts and Gerard (2004), pp. 289–322, sp. 302–303 and Pernice (2009), pp. 349–407, sp. 401; Gaudin (2004), pp. 541–557, sp. 549 ; Gaudin (2011), pp. 231–255, sp. 250.

important jurisprudence. Indeed, the Court innovated with the new concept of the preservation of *"the stability of the euro area as a whole"*. The recent comments issued by the academia[10] have not convincingly questioned, this very part of the judgment. This concept is considered by the Court as a new objective which justifies the adoption of a stability mechanism as the ESM Treaty. In that respect, there is no interference with the rules governing the two pillars of the EMU. As it results from the judgment, the new objective of the safeguard of *"the financial stability of the euro area as a whole"* constitutes the new arm of the EU and the Eurosystem to develop a full regime aimed at reinforcing the current framework of the EMU.

One could argue that the reasoning of the Court concerning the non-alteration of Article 122 para 2 TFEU on the basis that this provision concerns a provisional and not a permanent mechanism is not totally immune from criticism. This is because the regulation establishing the EFSM was based on this Article. Nevertheless, one should welcome the conclusion of the Court according to which, as a new objective, the safeguard *of "the financial stability of the euro area as a whole"* allowed Member States to establish a stability mechanism with a broad scope and without the infringement of this Article. There is no doubt that the scope of the assistance of Article 122 para 2 TFEU and the ESM are not comparable.

It must be added that with the proposal amending Article 136 para 3 TFEU, the Member States envisaged to put in place an important overall lending ceiling which is today set at euro 700 billion including the former intervention of the EFSM. This places the ESM on a footing more closely comparable to other international financial institutions such as the IMF. This is an element which could justify per se the amendment of Article 136 TFEU although this is not mentioned by the CJEU. In addition this element clearly distinguishes the ESM from the mechanism of the assistance under Article 122 para 2 TFEU.

As a general remark on this part of the Pringle judgment, one could maintain that the Court preferred to develop its reasoning on the basis of the new objective of *"the financial stability of the euro area as a whole"* and refused to elaborate a new jurisprudence with regard to Article 352 TFEU. It is not to be excluded that this Article could be used in the future, under certain circumstances, to establish a new stability mechanism at European level and to incorporate the ESM *"acquis"* within EU law.

In any event, it must be reminded that in the past, in the absence of the mechanism of a formal simplified revision procedure on the treaties, Article 352 TFEU was considered as a tool for the *"simplified"* revision of the community Treaties, in particular because the Council decided to act unanimously. The Court preferred to avoid any reference in that respect and to privilege the new procedure of Article 48 para 6 TEU. In the future, the interaction between Article 48 para 6 TEU and the revision clause of Article 352 TFEU might need to be clarified and this might be a subject for discussion during future Intergovernmental Conferences.

---

[10] See, for instance, Calliess (2013), pp. 97–105 sp. 99–100 and Frenz (2013), pp. 27–32, sp. 29.

References

Allemand F, Martucci F (2012) La nouvelle Gouvernance économique européenne II. CDE: 409–457
Calliess C (2013) Der ESM zwischen Luxemburg und Karlsruhe—Die Krise der Währungsunion als Bewährungsprobe der Rechtsgemeinschaft. NVwZ: 97–105
Frenz W (2013) ESM-Vertrag europarechtskonform!? EWS: 27–32
Gaudin H (2004) Révision des traités communautaires, révisions des constitutions nationales: recherches sur la symétrie d'un phénomène. In Mélanges en hommage à Guy Isaac: 50 ans de droit communautaire. T. 2 Presses de l'Université des sciences sociales, Toulouse pp 541–557
Gaudin H (2011) La procédure de révision des traités. In: Blanquet (ed) La prise de décision dans le système de l'union européenne. Bruxelles, Bruylant, pp 231–255
Lenaerts K, Gerard D (2004) The structure of the union according to the constitution for Europe: the emperor is getting dressed. ELR 29(3):289–322
Pernice I (2009) The treaty of Lisbon: multilevel constitutionalism in action. CJEL 3:349–407
Quesada LJ (2013) The revision procedures of the treaty. In: Blanke HJ, Mangiameli S (eds) The European union after Lisbon, constitutional basis, economic order and external action. Springer, Heidelberg, pp 323–342

Chapter 4
The ESM Treaty and European Law: A Necessary Coexistence

As a preliminary remark, the Pringle judgment is the first judgment in which the Court of Justice examined—in a preliminary ruling procedure—the compatibility with EU law of a Treaty, establishing a stability mechanism, concluded exclusively by the Member States without the involvement of the European Union. This is the consequence of the Court's choice to recognize its jurisdiction in order to interpret international agreements to which the European Union is not a contracting party.

Given also the fact that the Court recognized its jurisdiction to rule on the validity of the European Council Decision 2011/199 amending Article 136 TFEU, which provides also the possibility to establish a stability mechanism, the reasoning of the Court is in large part repetitive. Indeed, the Court used the same concepts, firstly in the framework of the examination of the conditions of the simplified revision procedure (Article 48 para 6 TEU), and secondly when the Member States established this mechanism via an international agreement. As will be examined below, in different parts of the Pringle judgment, the Court makes cross references to the main concept of its judgment, namely the safeguard of *"the stability of the euro area as a whole"*.

In any case, and despite the Court's stressing that its review does not cover the ESM treaty but rather the relevant provisions of primary EU law, it results clearly from the Pringle judgment that the Court examined the relevant provisions of the ESM treaty and grounded its reasoning on these provisions. As a result, in the future, international agreements concluded exclusively by the Member States, such as the Fiscal Compact or the EFSF framework agreement, could be subject to the review of the Court in the framework of a reference for a preliminary ruling. This is one of the main innovations of the Pringle judgment.

Further, the Court examined:

- Firstly, if by concluding the ESM Treaty the Member States have encroached upon the exclusive competence of the EU in the field of monetary policy and more generally the rules governing the exclusive competences of the EU such as determined by the Treaties (Sect. 4.1);

E. de Lhoneux and C. A. Vassilopoulos, *The European Stability Mechanism Before the Court of Justice of the European Union*, SpringerBriefs in Law,
DOI: 10.1007/978-3-319-01478-4_4, © The Author(s) 2014

- Secondly, if the conclusion of this treaty infringes the regime of the coordination of the economic policy of the Member States. In this respect, a detailed analysis is made on the main provisions of the economic pillar of the EMU (Articles 121–126 TFEU) (Sect. 4.2);
- Thirdly, if the allocation of some specific competences to the EU institutions (Commission, ECB, Court of Justice) in the framework of the ESM Treaty could infringe, inter alia, the principle of institutional balance, as provided for in the Treaties (Sect. 4.3);
- Finally, if the establishment of the ESM Treaty outside the EU legal order may have as a consequence that the ESM is removed from the scope of the Charter of fundamental rights of the EU (Charter), breaching Article 47 of this Charter, which guarantees that everyone enjoys the right to an effective judicial protection. It is the first time that the Court examined the impact of the Charter on the conclusion of an international agreement by certain Member States of the European Union (Sect. 4.4).

4.1 The Conclusion of the ESM Treaty by the Member States and the Exclusive Nature of the EU Competences

The Court examined firstly whether the conclusion of the ESM Treaty infringes the rules governing the exclusive competence of the EU in the area of monetary policy. In this respect, the Court refers in particular to Article 3 para 1c TFEU, 127 para 1 TFEU and 282 para 2 TFEU (Sect. 4.1.1).

The Court also interpreted Article 3 para 2 TFEU, under which the Union is to have exclusive competence for the conclusion of an international agreement when its conclusion, inter alia, may affect common rules or alter their scope. In this context, the Court of Justice examined if the conclusion of the ESM Treaty by the euro area Member States could infringe Article 3 para 2 TFEU, in particular because the EU institutions adopted common rules such as Regulation n°407/2010 establishing the EFSM (Sect. 4.1.2).

4.1.1 The Conclusion of the ESM Treaty and the Monetary Pillar of the EMU

Pursuant to Article 3 of the ESM Treaty, the purpose of the envisaged stability mechanism is to mobilize funding and provide stability support under strict conditionality. The same Article mentions that this purpose could be achieved to safeguard the financial stability of the euro area as a whole. On the other hand, Article 12 para 1 of the ESM Treaty refers to the same concept and focuses on the fact that the strict conditionality of the stability support of the ESM Treaty *"may range from a macro-economic adjustment program to continuous respect of pre-established eligibility conditions".*

The Court infers from these provisions that the purpose of the ESM Treaty is not to maintain price stability but rather to meet the financial requirements of the ESM Member States. In this respect, the Court concludes in para 96 of the judgment, that the ESM is not entitled to set the key interest rates for the euro area or to issue euro currency, while the financial assistance which the ESM grants to Member States must be entirely funded from paid-in capital or by the issuance of financial instruments as provided in Article 3 of the ESM Treaty. Based on its statement in para 56 ("safeguard of the stability of the euro area as a whole"), the Court adds that, *"even if the activities of the ESM might influence the rate of inflation, such an influence would constitute only the indirect consequence of the economic policy measures adopted"* (para 97).

Paragraph 56, together with paras 96 and 97, contains the fundamental elements that the Court uses to demonstrate that the ESM treaty could not infringe the monetary policy of the EU such as determined by the treaties. The reasoning of the Court can be subject to the following observations.

Firstly, it results from the considerations of the Court that the activities of the ESM could indirectly influence the inflation rate. However, for the Court, this indirect influence does not amount to an infringement of the fundamental rules governing monetary policy. This statement is based on the fact that this influence has only an *indirect* character. In the future, the Court will be invited possibly to further specify the meaning of such indirect character.

Secondly, the Court decided to build in the above mentioned paragraphs a new reasoning concerning the perimeter of the monetary policy and the rules possibly affecting this policy. In this respect, it results a contrario from the statement in para 97 of the judgment that a *direct* influence of economic policy measures on the rate of inflation could occur and, in this context, such direct influence could potentially violate the rules governing monetary policy. It could be observed that the Court did not develop further its reasoning avoiding therefore to engage in complex economic appraisals.

Indeed, a reasoning demonstrating the direct influence of economic policy measures on the inflation rate would imply for the Court to develop a complicated economic reasoning, which is a practice the Court does not normally follow in its case law. The fact that the subject matter of this case concerns an exclusive competence of the EU does not affect this consideration. In the present case, even if the Court did not refer mutatis mutandis to this case law, it seems to apply the same reasoning. It must be reminded that in its case law on the exclusive competence of the EU[1] such as, for instance, the common commercial policy (Article 3 para 1e) TFEU), the Court recognized that its review would be restricted in order to avoid complex economic appraisals (see e.g. competition cases).[2]

---

1 Gautier (2004), pp. 165–189, sp. 176.

2 See for instance, Case T-201/04, *Microsoft Corp. v Commission of the European Communities*, [2007] ECR II 3601, paras 87 and 379.

However, it must be stressed that, despite being an exclusive matter of EU competence, monetary policy enjoys a different status than the other 'classic' EU exclusive competences. Indeed, monetary policy involves a number of distinct legal, financial and economic features that make it unique. Therefore, the prudent approach used by the Court, and in particular its choice not to intervene in this field, must be appreciated.

4.1.2 The Conclusion of the ESM Treaty by the Member States and the Possibility to Affect Common Rules or Alter Their Scope

According to Article 3 para 2 TFEU, the EU has exclusive competence to conclude an international agreement when its conclusion may affect common rules or alter their scope. In this regard, it was submitted before the Court that the conclusion of the ESM Treaty by the Member States shall be prohibited to the extent that this agreement may affect common rules. The referring court requested the CJEU precisely to rule on this issue given the fact that ESM took over the tasks conferred on the EFSF and the EFSM.

Concerning, firstly, the EFSF, the CJEU rejects this argumentation considering that, since the EFSF was established outside the framework of the Union, the transfer to the ESM of the tasks conferred on the EFSF is not such as to affect common rules or alter their scope (para 102).

Indeed, the mere fact that the EFSF, a "société anonyme" incorporated in Luxembourg, was established outside the framework of the European Union is a convincing argument in favour of this view. The Court could have added, in order to strengthen its reasoning, that the EFSF framework agreement is also an agreement established outside the framework of the EU. In this context, there is no possibility that the conclusion of the ESM Treaty by the Member States could affect common rules or alter their scope.

Concerning, secondly, the EFSM, the Court could not develop the same reasoning because the EFSM is established by Regulation n°407/2010 and the conclusion of the ESM Treaty could affect or alter the scope of the common rules provided by this regulation.

It could be argued that there is a major difference between Regulation n°407/2010 and the ESM Treaty, namely that the former applies to the EU, whereas the latter applies only to the euro area. Also, the mechanism established by Regulation n°407/2010 (the EFSM) was financed exclusively by the European Union budget.[3] On this basis, given the fundamental difference regarding the

[3] See Allemand and Martucci (2012), pp. 409–457, sp. 429 and Dechâtre (2011), pp. 303–342, sp. 334 and the bibliography mentioned in footnote 162 of the latter Article.

scope and the origin of the financial resources engaged respectively by the EFSM and the ESM, it was impossible to argue that the mechanism envisaged by the ESM could affect or alter the scope of the common rules.

The Court did not develop any argument on the above mentioned elements and stated that, even if it is apparent from recital 1 of the Preamble to the ESM Treaty that the ESM will assume the tasks allocated temporarily to the EFSM, the establishment of the ESM does not affect the power of the European Union to grant, on the basis of Article 122 para 2 TFEU, ad hoc financial assistance to a Member State when it is found that such Member State is in difficulty (paras 103–104). For the Court, since Article 122 para 2 TFEU (or any other EU and FEU provision) does not confer a specific power on the European Union to establish a permanent stability mechanism, Member States are entitled, on the basis of the Treaties, to act in this area (para 105).

It results from the reasoning of the Court that the action the Member States took in the field of financial assistance by concluding the ESM Treaty could not infringe the *ad hoc* temporary measures which the European Union can adopt on the basis of Article 122 para 2 TFEU. For the Court, the extremely large scope of the stability mechanism established by the ESM Treaty could not be based on an EU Treaty provision, or on specific provisions such as Article 122 para 2 TFEU, which has an extremely restrictive scope. In this context, it is impossible to establish that the ESM Treaty affects or in any case alters the scope of the common rules contained in the EFSM regulation. The fact that the mechanism established by the EFSM covers the European Union, cannot be considered as the main element on which the Court could base the conclusion that common rules are not affected or altered.

The reasoning of the Court is certainly convincing and, in any case, as observed by Professor Louis, Article 122 para 2 TFEU does not mention the forms of the financial assistance.[4] Probably, in order to strengthen its reasoning, the Court could have added that the actions of the Member States via the ESM Treaty have a complementary character to the common rules, while not aiming at affecting the common rules provided by the EFSM regulation. It was however difficult for the Court to develop a reasoning based on the complementary nature of these interventions (ad hoc assistance/permanent financial assistance) without putting in evidence the impact of the ESM provisions on the common rules or the affectation of these rules.

Nevertheless, the Court indirectly recognized that it is possible that the EU institutions and the Member States act in a complementary fashion in the field of financial assistance. Indeed, in para 106, the Court stated that the conclusion of the ESM treaty did not jeopardize the objective of Article 122 para 2 TFEU, but at the same time pointed out that such conclusion does not prevent *"the Union from*

[4] Louis (2010), pp. 971–986, sp. 983.

exercising its own competences in the defense of the common interest". To this purpose, the Court refers to the *Open skies* case cited above.

The CJEU concludes that the ESM Treaty does not jeopardize *"in any way"* the objective pursued by Article 122 para 2 TFEU or by the Council Regulation n°407/2010 establishing the ESFM (para 106). The Court also stated that the ESM Treaty could not affect the temporary measures adopted in the framework of the ESM regulation. Perhaps the Court could have added that the ESM Treaty could be considered as a complementary intervention not affecting or altering the scope of the common rules. However, in this part of the judgment the Court preferred to remain silent and did not nuance its reasoning.

4.2 The Conclusion of the ESM Treaty and the Economic Pillar of the EMU

As a preliminary remark, it must be observed that, in general, the Court interpreted the primary EU law provisions constituting the economic pillar of the EMU on different levels. For instance, when examining the conditions laid down in Article 48 para 6 TEU, the Court analyzed if the amendment of the treaties attributing the Member States a competence to establish a stability mechanism is compatible with the regime of the economic pillar of the EMU such as provided for by the Treaties. The Court reminds also the substance of its reasoning from a different perspective, that is to say asking itself if the ESM treaty, which establishes the financial stability mechanism, is compatible with the same provisions. In this respect, we observe that the Court was obliged to make cross references to its case law and, as a consequence, its reasoning is at times repetitive.

Nonetheless, the Court did not have the opportunity to analyze if the ESM Treaty is compatible with the provisions of the economic pillar of the EMU, especially because the proposed amendment of Article 136 TFEU on the basis of Article 48 para 6 had not entered into force and the only legal instrument that was discussed was the ESM Treaty. In this context, the Court developed, for the first time in its case law, its own legal doctrine concerning the interpretation of the main provisions of the economic pillar of the EMU and that in relation to the provisions of the ESM Treaty (paras 108–147).

On the basis of the above, the Court examined four main issues:

- *Firstly*, whether the ESM Treaty encroaches upon the competence conferred on the Union institutions for the coordination of the economic policy such as determined by Articles 2 para 3, 119–121 and 126 TFEU (Sect. 4.2.1).
- *Secondly*, whether the ESM Treaty encroaches upon the competence attributed to the Council by 122 TFEU to adopt the appropriate measures if several difficulties arise in the supply of certain products (para 1) and in case of granting of financial assistance (para 2) (Sect. 4.2.2).

- *Thirdly*, whether the conclusion of the ESM circumvents Article 123 TEFU which prohibits the ECB and the NCBs from granting overdraft facilities or any other credit facility to public authorities and bodies of the EU and of the Member States and purchasing directly their debt instruments (Sect. 4.2.3).
- *Fourthly*, whether an international agreement such as the ESM Treaty is in breach of the so-called "no bail-out clause" provided for in Article 125 TFEU (Sect. 4.2.4).

4.2.1 The ESM Treaty and the Perimeter of Economic Policies Coordination (Articles 2 para 3, 119–121 and 126 TFEU)

The national court, referring to the arguments of the parties, claimed that Articles 2 para 3, 119–121 and 126 TFEU confer on the Union the competence for the coordination of the economic policies of the Member States, and in this respect the permanent stability mechanism put in place by the ESM Treaty encroaches upon the competence of the European Union. In particular, the need to modify Article 136 TFEU through the European Council Decision 2011/199 itself demonstrates that a permanent stability mechanism could not be easily established under the existing legal framework provided for in the Treaties.

Before developing a detailed reasoning, in this part of the judgment the Court reminds the content of para 68 of the judgment! following which the Member States have the power to conclude between themselves an agreement for the establishment of a stability mechanism such as the ESM Treaty, provided that the commitment undertaken by the Member states parties to such agreement is consistent with European Union law (para 109). In sum, the Court reminds that, even if the Member States have the competence to enter into an international agreement in order to establish a permanent stability mechanism, this power should not be used to circumvent Member States' obligations deriving from European Union law.

Examining the subject matter of the ESM Treaty, the Court preliminarily observed that the ESM does not concern the coordination of the economic policy of the Member States, but rather constitutes a financing mechanism (Para 110), because, as results from Article 3 and 12 para 1 of the ESM Treaty, its purpose is to mobilize funding and to provide financial stability support to the ESM Member States, which are experiencing or are threatened by severe financing problems. For the Court, the subject matter of the ESM Treaty does not fall within the regime of the cooperation policy.

Examining the provisions of the ESM Treaty, the Court reminded that under Articles 3, 12 paras 1 and 13 para 3 first subparagraph of the ESM Treaty, the financial assistance provided to an ESM Member State is subject to strict conditionality, which can take the form of a macro-economic adjustment program.

However, this conditionality does not constitute an instrument for the coordination of the economic policy of the Member States, but is rather meant to ensure that the activities of the ESM are compatible with the measures adopted by the European Union, and inter alia with Article 125 TFEU (no bail-out clause) (Para 111).

In order to strengthen its reasoning the Court adds that the second subparagraph of Article 13(3) of the ESM Treaty expressly provides that the conditions of any stability support are to be fully consistent with the measures of economic policy coordination provided for in the Treaties. Further, according to the Court, it is apparent from Article 13(4) of the ESM Treaty that the Commission is to check, before signing the Memorandum of Understanding defining the conditionality attached to any stability support, that the conditions imposed are fully consistent with the measures of economic policy coordination (para 112).

Certainly, according to the Court, the financial assistance of the ESM intervention is subject to the so-called "strict conditionality". However, the Court points out that this conditionality ensures that the activities of the ESM are compatible with the measures adopted by the EU institutions precisely in the field of the coordination of the economic policies of the Member States. In fact, the conditionality of the financial assistance implies a necessary action of the Member States which is in line with the EU coordination rules. This "conditionality" is precisely the appropriate tool ensuring that Member State action does not infringe the legal framework of the coordination of the economic policies of the Member States. Possibly for this reason, in para 111 of the judgment, the Court refers to Article 125 TFEU.

However, one could argue that the conditionality such as determined by the Court could limit the scope of the ESM financial assistance. Indeed, it could be argued that not any financial assistance is covered by the intervention of the stability mechanism, but only the assistance which is in line with the rules on the coordination of the economic policies. In this context, this conditionality could be possibly understood as an instrument of the coordination of the economic policy of the Member States.

The Court considered, nevertheless, that the conditional financial assistance ensures that the regime of the EU coordination rules is not affected and that conditionality is not an instrument of the coordination of the economic policies of the Member States. Under these conditions, according to the Pringle judgment, there is no incompatibility between the ESM intervention and the EU coordination rules. Perhaps the Court could have explained further why the conditionality could not constitute or be assimilated to an instrument for the coordination of the economic policies of Member States, because one could argue that this conditionality proves that the action of the Member States is in the field of the coordination of economic policies as it is also attested by the action of the Member States within the STACOG Treaty.

In addition, it must be reminded that for the contracting parties of the ESM and the STACOG Treaty, there is a clear interaction of these two instruments which could be interpreted as the evidence that the so called conditionality is in fact a specific mechanism of the coordination of the economic policies of the Member States. Indeed, this is confirmed by recital 5 of the ESM Treaty, according to which the granting of financial assistance in the framework of the new program under the ESM will be conditional on the ratification of the STACOG Treaty. In this respect, in its judgment the Court could have developed its reasoning further, because it could be argued that it results clearly from the ESM and the STACOG Treaty, which are not acts of EU law, that the Member States established complementary rules on the coordination of their economic policies in addition to the existing EU rules.

Finally, the argument that the ESM Treaty affects the competence of the Council to issue recommendations to the Member States on the basis of Article 126 TFEU (excessive deficit procedure) was easily overcome by the Court, firstly because, undoubtedly, the ESM is not called upon to issue such recommendations and, secondly, because this treaty provides expressly that the ESM Member States which receive financial assistance must be consistent with all recommendations (Para 113). This reasoning must be welcomed, because, as pointed out by the Court, not only does the ESM Treaty not provide a mechanism to adopt recommendations in this field, but also, on the contrary, it stresses the necessity to comply with Article 126 TFEU.

Examining the analysis of the Court on the interpretation of the provisions of the economic pillar in the framework of the conditions amending Article 136 TFEU, the following observations must be made.

The Court considered, firstly, that the envisaged stability mechanism falls within the field of economic policy; secondly, that the stability mechanism does not infringe the regime of coordination provided for by the treaties, and, thirdly, that the financial assistance granted by the stability mechanism is compatible with the coordination regime because this assistance is conditional. For the Court, this conditionality is not an instrument of the coordination rules of the economic policy for which EU law conferred in fact a competence to the EU institutions. However, as demonstrated by its reasoning, the conditionality of the assistance is related directly to the respect of the EU coordination rules. Save its last step (conditionality), which could have been strengthened, the reasoning of the Court must be in general welcomed.

4.2.2 The ESM Treaty and the Assistance to a Member State (Article 122 TFEU)

As a preliminary remark, it must be observed that the Court analyzed the provisions of Article 122 para 2 TFEU on different levels. Firstly, to point out that the European Union has not a residual competence in the field of financial assistance in order to establish a stability mechanism as provided by the European Council Decision 2011/199. Secondly, to assess whether the conclusion of the ESM could affect or alter the common rules adopted on the basis of Article 122 para 2 TFEU, that is to say Regulation n°407/2010 establishing the EFSM. In the above case, the Court pointed out that Article 122 para 2 TFEU did not confer any competence on the EU to establish a permanent stability mechanism and that the common rules adopted on the basis of this article (Regulation n°407/2010) have an extremely narrow scope. Thirdly, in addition to the above mentioned conclusions, the Court was invited to examine whether the conclusion of the ESM Treaty per se could infringe Article 122 TFEU.

Concerning Article 122 para 1 TFEU, this provision provides that the Council in a spirit of solidarity between Member States may decide upon measures appropriate to the economic situation, in particular if several difficulties arise in the supply of certain products. On the basis of the wording of this Article the Court pointed out that this provision does not constitute an appropriate legal basis for any financial assistance and that the envisaged stability mechanism such as provided by the ESM Treaty does not encroach upon the powers conferred by this Article to the Council (para 106).

The reasoning of the Court does not require any specific comment as the Court explains that Article 122 para 1 TFEU has nothing in common with a stability mechanism such as the ESM.

Concerning Article 122 para 2 TFEU, the referring judge requested the Court to examine the compatibility of the ESM Treaty with this Article in a different context, that is to say whether this provision exhaustively defines the exceptional circumstances in which it is possible to grant financial assistance to Member States and whether only the EU institutions are empowered to grant financial assistance.

When the Court examines the conditions regarding the amendment of Article 136 TFEU, it states that the envisaged stability mechanism does not infringe the EU rules provided for in Article 122 para 2 TFEU, because the new stability mechanism has a permanent character in contrast to the temporary nature of the tools foreseen in this Article. Furthermore, the Court pointed out that the envisaged stability mechanism ensures the preservation of "the stability of the euro area as a whole", thus having a larger scope than that of Article 122 para 2 TFEU.

One could have expected that, in this part of the judgment, the Court would restate this reasoning, concluding that the Member States had the competence to establish a mechanism such as that provided by the ESM Treaty, and then would determine the content of the exceptional circumstances justifying the application of Article 122 para 2 TFEU. These are very important issues, because the question was whether this provision could be used when a Member State is very close to a situation of selected default or default. Having in mind also that Regulation n°407/2010 establishing the EFSM is based on Article 122 para 2 TFEU, one could think that the Court would clarify the conditions of the application of this Article.

The Court did not follow this path, and stressed, *firstly,* that Article 122 para 2 TFEU concerns solely the financial assistance granted by the Union and not by the Member States (para 118); *secondly*, that the exercise of this competence by the EU is not affected by the establishment of a stability mechanism by the Member States such the ESM (para 119); and, *thirdly*, that Article 122 para 2 TFEU does not confer on the EU an exclusive competence to grant financial assistance to a Member State (para 120). There is no indication in this part of the judgment about the meaning of the exceptional circumstances justifying the application of Article 122 para 2 TFEU.

The Court seems to recognize that a joint action in the field of financial assistance could be put in place by EU institutions and Member States on different levels. It seems that for the Court the action of EU institutions under Article 122 para 2 TFEU has a restricted scope and a limited perspective *rationae temporis,* whereas the Member States stability mechanism (ESM Treaty) has a larger scope, as determined by the new concept of the safeguard "*of the stability of the euro area as a whole*".

The scope of the ESM assistance is larger than the perimeter of the financial assistance which may be granted under certain conditions on the basis of Article 122 para 2 TFEU. Interestingly, however, the Court failed to recall the objective of the ESM (safeguard "*of the stability of the euro area as a whole*") which was one of the bases of the first part of the Pringle judgment. Under those conditions, the Court concluded that the Member States remain free to establish a stability mechanism, provided however that in its operation this mechanism complies with EU law and, in particular, with measures adopted by the Union in the field of the coordination of economic policies. For the Court, the ESM provisions (inter alia Article 13) are intended to ensure that any financial assistance granted by the ESM will be consistent with such coordinated measures (para 121).

In this paragraph, the Court recognizes once more that the ESM intervention (financial assistance granted) shall comply with EU coordination rules. Here lays the main peculiarity of the Court's reasoning in this part of the judgment: on the one hand the Court recognized the possible joint action of the Member States and of the EU in the field of financial assistance, on the other hand it stressed that the ESM financial assistance shall be conditional, that is to say compatible with EU coordinated measures. An alternative approach could have been for the Court to simply recognize the existence of a joint action in the field of financial assistance and the fact that, in any case, EU measures under Article 122 para 2 TFEU and ESM interventions have a different scope.

The Court finally reminds in para 120 that nothing in Article 122 TFEU indicates that the EU has exclusive competence to grant financial assistance to a Member State. This clarification allows to better understand the reasoning of the Court, although legally speaking it was not necessary to mention it, as Article 122 TFEU is part of the economic pillar of the EMU and therefore is not among the provisions of the Treaties which confer exclusive competence on the EU.

One could regret that, in this part of the judgment, once again the Court did not take position on the meaning of the exceptional circumstances to which Article 122 para 2 TFEU refers. However, given the context of the review of the Court and in particular the interpretation of this provision by national judges, the Court adopted a prudent approach and avoided any controversy with the national court, focusing on the strict interpretation of this provision, under which the competence of the EU to grant financial assistance on the basis of Article 122 para 2 TFEU does not affect the establishment of a stability mechanism by the Member States.

4.2.3 The ESM Treaty and the Monetary Financing Prohibition (Article 123 TFEU)

The referring judge asked the CJEU whether the conclusion of the ESM Treaty is not intended to circumvent the monetary financing prohibition laid down in Article 123 TFEU. Indeed, it was argued before the Court that some provisions of the ESM treaty circumvent this prohibition, according to which *"overdraft facilities or any other type of credit facility with the ECB or with the NCB in favour of Union Institutions, bodies, offices or agencies, central governments, regional, local or other public authorities, other bodies governed by public law, or public undertakings of Member States shall be prohibited, as shall the purchase directly from them by the ECB or NCB of debt instruments".*

Before examining the position of the Court, it must be reminded that since the first agreement concerning the Greek debt in 2010, the question was whether the purchasing by the Eurosystem of the bonds on the secondary market circumvented the prohibition provided in Article 123 para 1 TFEU. In that respect, arguments are based inter alia on the recital 7 of the Regulation n°3603/93,[5] according to which *"purchases made on the secondary market must not be used to circumvent the objective of Article [104 EC] 123 TFEU"*; and on Article 18 para 1 of the Statute, following which *"in order to achieve the objective of the ESCB and to carry out its tasks, the ECB and the NCBs may operate in the financial markets by buying and selling outright or under repurchase agreements and by lending or borrowing claims and marketable instruments".*

In the Pringle judgment, the Court had the chance to clarify the controversy concerning the scope of the above mentioned prohibition, that it to say whether Article 123 TFEU prohibits purchases over the primary and/or secondary market.[6] It should further be reminded that the disagreements concerning the interpretation of this provision were also of political nature and the parties before the CJEU developed a full argumentation inviting the Court to take position. This was all the more necessary because the ECB has strengthened its position on this matter adopting the regime of Outright Monetary Transactions (OMT) which replaced the Securities Market Program (SMP) with the peculiarity that OMT transactions are unlimited, unlike the SMP program providing for a ceiling.[7]

Given the sensitivity of the issue, the Court prudently preferred not to take an express standing regarding these arguments, again to the surprise of the

[5] Council Regulation (EC) n°3603/93 of 13 December 1993 specifying definitions for the application of prohibition referred to in Articles 104 and 104b (1) of the Treaty (OJ L 332, p. 1).

[6] See inter alia Tomuschat (2012), pp. 1431–1434, sp. 1433 and Ahari (2012), pp. 878–880 sp. 879; See also Wendel (2013), pp. 21–52, sp. 49. See in a similar context Santulli (2011), pp. 833–851, sp. 843.

[7] Sester (2012a), pp. 80–90 sp. 82 and Sester (2012b), pp 156–178 sp. 168; see also Schneider (2013), pp 53–74, sp. 74 point D. See also Cecchini (2012), pp. 122–131, sp 126.

academia.[8] The Court preferred to follow a strict interpretation of the provision of Article 123 para 1 TFEU, engaging in a two steps reasoning.

Firstly, the Court examined the scope ratione "personae" of the monetary financing prohibition. In this respect, it observed that Article 123 para 1 TFEU is addressed specifically to the ECB and central banks of the Member States. Consequently, it concluded that the grant of financial assistance by one Member State or a group of Member States to another Member State is not covered by the monetary financing prohibition provided for in this article (para 125).

The Court had to examine whether the financial assistance granted via the ESM is in fact granted by the Eurosystem. Examining the relevant provisions of the ESM Treaty, the Court observed, firstly, that according to Article 3 of the ESM Treaty, it is the ESM that raises funds by issuing financial instruments or entering into financial or other agreements or arrangements with ESM members; secondly, that pursuant to Article 12 para 1, it is the ESM that provides stability support to an ESM Member State and, thirdly, that according to Article 13, it is the ESM that decides to grant a stability support to an ESM member in the form of a financial assistance facility. For the Court, it clearly results from the above mentioned provisions of the ESM Treaty that it is the ESM that grants the financial assistance and not the ECB or the NCBs (para 126).

There is no doubt that the Court follows a strict interpretation of Article 123 para 1 TFEU, thus demonstrating a realistic view of the problem. The Court also decided to refer only to the provisions concerned by the present litigation.

It must be observed, however, that in the above mentioned para 126 of the Pringle judgment the Court recognized that via the ESM Treaty it is in fact Member States who grant financial assistance. The Court adds that even if the Member States are acting via the ESM, they are not derogating from the prohibition laid down in Article 123 para 1 TFEU because in any case Article 123 TFEU is not addressed to Member States.

Secondly, the Court examined if the financial instruments used by the Member States in the ESM framework are covered by the monetary policy prohibition. The Court, once again following a strict interpretation of Article 123 para 1 TFEU, observed that there is no ground to consider that the funds provided by the ESM members to the ESM might be derived from the financial instruments prohibited by Article 123 para 1 TFEU (para 127).

It is not certain whether this second clarification without any detail was really necessary to demonstrate that the prohibition laid down in Article 123 para 1 TFEU is not affected by the conclusion of the ESM Treaty. Indeed, only the first consideration regarding the fact that in any case this prohibition is not addressed to the Member States but to the ESCB/Eurosystem was sufficient to reject the claim developed before the referring court. In addition, the Court's second step argumentation seems to envisage in the framework of the ESM Treaty that there are some

[8] See, in particular, Calliess (2013), pp. 97–105, sp. 103; Frenz (2013), pp. 27–32, sp. 30.

financial instruments which could be considered as prohibited by Article 123 para 1 TFEU, regardless of the consideration that it is the ESM that grants assistance to Member States and not the ESCB/Eurosystem.

Finally, the Court did not draw any argumentation from para 2 of Article 123 TFEU which contains the exception to the monetary financing prohibition. According to this provision (Article 123 para 2 TFEU, indicating that para 1 does not apply to publicly owned credit institutions which, in the context of the supply of reserves by central banks, shall be given the same treatment by NCBs and the ECB as private credit institutions), as results also from the second paragraph of Article 123 TFEU, even in the case of derogation to this prohibition the assistance is still granted by the ECB and the relevant central banks and not by the Member States.

4.2.4 The ESM Treaty andthe No Bail-Out Clause (Article 125 TFEU)

The CJEU was also invited to take position on the question whether the conclusion of the ESM Treaty breaches the no bail-out clause provided for in Article 125 TFEU. Pursuant to this Article, the Union and/or the Member States *"shall not be liable for assume the commitments"* of central government, regional, local or other public authorities, other bodies governed by public law, or public undertakings of the Member States without prejudice to mutual financial guarantees for the joint execution of a specific project.

Before analyzing the position of the Court, it must be noted that the Pringle litigation gave the Court the opportunity to interpret for the first time the much discussed[9] provision of the so called "no bail-out clause". This article is the centre of the doctrinal controversy[10] concerning its scope and more generally the interaction of this clause with the other provisions of the economic pillar of the EMU, such as Articles 122, 123 and 124 TFEU.[11]

It has been questioned whether the no bail-out clause has an absolute character or if it lends itself to a wide interpretation[12] that allows to consider Article 125 TFEU as subject to certain exceptions. One of the elements corroborating the latter option is the wording used by this Article, according to which the no bail-out

---

[9] See Dehousse (1995), p. 243.

[10] See inter alia de Gregorio Merino (2012), pp. 1613–1646, sp. 1625; Louis (2010), pp. 971–986, sp. 977; Häde (2009), pp. 399–403, sp. 402; Hentschelmann (2011), pp. 282–312 sp. 301; Herrmann (2010), pp. 413–416, sp. 416; Mayer (2012), pp. 124–136, sp. 127; Middleton (2012), pp. 422–425; Seidel (2011), pp. 529–530; Tomkin (2013), pp. 169–189, sp. 187.

[11] Louis (2009), pp. 95–97. See also in relation to the CACs Sester (2011), pp. 1057–1066, sp. 1062 point b).

[12] See in that respect, Martucci (2010), p. 883; Allemand (2012), p. 553–594, sp. 581.

clause is "without prejudice to mutual financial guarantees for the joint execution of a specific project". It results from the terms used in this provision that the authors of the Treaties recognize that the no bail-out clause is not absolute.

In addition, the authors of the treaties chose in Article 125 TFEU a more flexible wording whose interpretation can be wide (*"shall not be liable for assume the commitments")* compared to the strict wording used in Articles 123 TFEU and 124 TFEU which reefers expressly to a "prohibition".

In the same context, it is admitted, like the prohibition of Articles 123 and 124 TFEU, that Article 125 TFEU must be examined in relation to the ad hoc regime of the budgetary discipline (Article 126 TFEU)[13] and that the no bail-out clause must not be invoked in order to avoid the adoption of measures aiming to ensure the safeguard of the stability of the euro area. It could also be argued that the conclusion that the no bail-out clause has no absolute character can be drawn from Article 122 TFEU, which at primary law level provides a peculiar regime of financial assistance. Finally, it is argued that the operations covered by the no bail-out clause concerned only guarantee operations and not any possible measure aiming to help the concerned Member States to face the hostility of the markets.

Before all these arguments, the Court needed to structure the doctrinal debate and to develop a broad analysis of the conditions for the application of Article 125 TFEU. That was all the more necessary given the previous practice in this area. Indeed, the tools adopted to help Greece to avoid defaulting (Greek loan facility) are considered contrary to Article 125 TFEU[14] despite the political effort of the Member States to ensure that the no bail-out clause is not breached. In the same line, it is also argued that the EFSF, despite being formally a *"société anonyme de droit luxembourgeois"*, is in fact as an indirect mechanism put in place in order to allow the financing of the Member States in difficulty, contrary to the no bail-out clause.

The Court stated that it results from the wording used in Article 125 TFEU, and in particular from the terms *"not be liable"*, that this Article is not aimed at prohibiting the Member States from grating *any form of financial assistance* to any other Member State. In order to strengthen this statement the Court pointed out that such reading of Article 125 TFEU is supported by other provisions relating to the economic policy, in particular Article 122 TFEU and 123 TFEU (paras 130 and 131).

On the one hand, Article 122 para 2 TFEU provides that the EU can grant ad hoc financial assistance to a Member State in some particular and exceptional circumstances. For the Court, if Article 125 TFEU prohibited any financial assistance, "*Article 122 would have had to state that it derogated from Article 125*". On the other hand, the Court strengthened this reasoning, observing that Article 123 TFEU employs a wording which is "*stricter than the one used in a no-bail out clause in Article 125*". In that conditions, the Court concludes that "*the difference in the wording used in the latter article supports the view that the prohibition*

[13] See Louis (2004) n°125 et suiv.

[14] See, inter alia, recently Palmostorfer (2012), pp. 771–784, sp. 778 and the cited legal doctrine.

stated is not intended to prohibit any financial assistance whatever to a Member State" (paras 131 and 132).

It results clearly from the above mentioned paragraphs of the judgment that the Court interpreted Article 125 TFEU broadly. In this respect, the Court focused, firstly, on the circumstance that the prohibition laid down in Article 125 TFEU is not absolute and secondly that such Article did not exclude the possibility for the Member States to grant financial assistance to other Member States.

In this context, it was necessary for the Court to determine which forms of financial assistance are compatible with Article 125 TFEU and what is the objective pursued by this article. Below we analyze the position of the Court regarding the objectives pursued by Article 125 TFEU.

On the basis of the preparatory work relating to the Treaty of Maastricht which inserted in primary EU law Article 125 TFEU (former Article 104b of the European Community Treaty which became Article 103 EC), the Court considered that the aim of Article 125 TFEU is to ensures to ensure that the Member States follow a sound budgetary policy and the prohibition laid down by this article ensures that Member States are subject to the logic of the market where they enter into debt in order to maintain a budgetary discipline. In this respect, according to the Court, *"compliance with such discipline contributes to the attainment of a higher objective, namely maintaining the financial stability of the monetary union"* (para 135).

In para 135 of the judgment, the Court mentions a new concept, that of *"the financial stability of the monetary union"*. The Court drew this concept from the preparatory works related to the Treaty of Maastricht. However, the association of the financial assistance to *"the monetary union"* could create some confusion on the exact meaning of this objective. This is because, inter alia, Article 125 TFEU is a provision concerning the economic pillar of the EMU and not the monetary pillar. In addition, this new concept must be articulated with the objective to preserve the "*stability of the euro area as a whole*" (para 56). In this respect, the Court gives some indications in the following paragraphs of the judgment.

Indeed, with reference to the new objective of the *"financial stability of the monetary union"*, the Court stated that Article 125 TFEU prohibits the Union and the Member States from granting financial assistance, as a result of which the incentive for the recipient Member State to conduct a sound budgetary policy is diminished. In contrast, this Article does not prohibit the granting of financial assistance by one or more Member States which remain responsible for their commitment vis-à-vis its creditors, provided that the conditions attached to this assistance are such as to prompt such Member State to implement a sound budgetary policy (paras 136 and 137). In this respect, the Court reminds that the financial assistance, by means of a stability mechanism such as the ESM, is compatible with Article 125 TFEU when, on the one hand, it is indispensable for the safeguarding of the financial stability of the euro area as a whole and, on the other hand, it is subject to strict conditions (principle of conditionality).[15]

[15] Louis (2010), pp. 971–986, sp. 979.

As results from the above mentioned paragraphs, the prohibition of Article 125 TFEU aims to ensure the *"financial stability of the monetary union"* and, as an exception to this prohibition, financial assistance could be granted by the Member States to other Member States when this assistance aims to safeguard the financial stability of the euro area as a whole and when it is "conditional". It is interesting to observe that the Court combines these two different concepts. However, it is not sure whether the two concepts correspond to two different objectives.

On the basis of the above considerations and in order to demonstrate that the financial stability envisaged by the ESM Treaty does not affect the no bail-out clause the Court rejects the argumentations developed by the parties.

Examining Articles 14–18 of the ESM Treaty, the Court <u>firstly</u> considers that the ESM will not act as guarantor of the debts of the recipient Member States (para 138).

Pursuant to Article 14 of the ESM Treaty, the ESM (Board of Governors) may decide to grant precautionary financial assistance in the form of a precautionary conditioned credit line or in the form of an enhanced conditioned credit line. Article 15 of the ESM Treaty, para 1, provides that the ESM may decide to grant financial assistance through loans to an ESM member for the specific purpose of recapitalizing the financial institution of the concerned ESM Member State. Article 16 provides that the ESM may grant financial assistance in the form of a loan in accordance to the principle of strict conditionality such as it is provided in Article 12 (ESM loans).

The Court observes that the grant of financial assistance according to those provisions does not imply that the ESM will assume the debts of the recipient Member State. In this respect, the Court justifies its reasoning on the basis that such financial assistance amounts to the creation of a new debt owed to the ESM. The assistance granted by the ESM on the basis of Articles 14–16 of the ESM Treaty must in any case be paid to the ESM, including an appropriate margin (para 139).

This interpretation of the ESM Treaty provisions is in line with the interpretation of the no-bail out clause because precisely the Member States concerned remain responsible for their commitment to their creditors. In addition, the principle of conditionality which applies to all the financial interventions on the basis of these articles ensures that the conditions attached to the financial assistance prompt the recipient Member State to implement a sound budgetary policy. The Court's reasoning is very consistent and therefore must be welcomed.

The Court also used this reasoning when examining the conformity with EU law of the regime of the ESM market support facility such as provided for in Articles 17 and 18 of the ESM Treaty. In this respect, it must be reminded that pursuant to Article 17, the ESM may decide to arrange for the purchase of the bonds of an ESM member on the primary market. Article 18 provides for the possibility for the ESM to arrange for operations on the secondary market in relation to the bonds of an ESM member.

Concerning the purchase by the ESM of the bonds issued by an ESM member *in the primary market* (Article 17 ESM Treaty), the Court considered that this intervention in the primary market is comparable to the granting of a loan (para 140) which is subject to the specific conditions (conditionality) provided for by the ESM. With this intervention in the primary market, the ESM becomes a new creditor for the concerned Member State. The Court concludes that under those conditions, the ESM does not assume the debt of the recipient Member State.

The Court has made an important effort in order to demonstrate that the regime of the primary market support facility provided for in the ESM Treaty is in line with the no bail-out clause. Indeed, by purchasing bonds issued by ESM members on the primary market, the ESM formally *"does not assume the debts of the recipient Member State"*.

However, one could argue that the proceeds resulting from the bonds issued on the primary market by the concerned ESM Member State aim to service other outstanding debt by this State. It is precisely the need to honor the sovereign debt that leads a Member State to issue new bonds and request a primary market support facility. In sum, the Court grounds its reasoning on an argument which is formally correct, but which, from a practical point of view, does not mirror the economic status of the sovereign debt of the Member States concerned.

Concerning the purchase *on the secondary market* of bonds issued by an ESM Member State (Article 18 ESM Treaty), the Court stated in the Pringle judgment (para 141) that the issuing Member States remain solely answerable to repay the debts in question. The Court illustrated its reasoning in para 141 as follows: *"the fact that the ESM as the purchaser on that market of bonds issued by an ESM Member pays a price to the holder of those bonds, who is the creditor of the issuing ESM Member, does not mean that the ESM becomes responsible for the debt of that ESM Member to that creditor. That price may be significantly different from the value of the claims contained in those bonds, since the price depends on the rules of supply and demand on the secondary market of bonds issued by the ESM Member concerned"*.

Again, as was the case in the paragraph on the intervention on the primary market, the statement of the Court is correct, because the intervention on the secondary market does not modify the status of the issuing Member State as a debtor. The only modification concerns the creditors and, such as provided by the ESM Treaty, this intervention on the secondary market is justified by the need to prevent contagions and by the existence of exceptional financial market circumstances and risks to financial stability. However, the intervention of the ESM in the secondary market allows the debtor ESM Member State, in practice, to manage its debt outside the original legal framework governing the issuance.

Secondly, the Court points out that the ESM Treaty does not provide that the stability support will be granted as soon as a Member State is experiencing difficulties in obtaining financing in the market. For the Court, the stability support may be granted to the ESM members only when such support is indispensable to safeguard the stability of the euro area as a whole and the grant of such support is subject to strict conditionality (para 142).

This was perhaps not necessary for the Court to add, as, despite the statement of the Court, one could argue that the stability support of the ESM is in fact an instrument in order get around the difficulties which a Member State faces in receiving funds from the market. In addition, it is precisely the financial assistance of the ESM which allows the Member States to have a sound budgetary policy in order to get back to the market.

Finally, the Court examined whether the rules relating to capital calls stated in Article 25 para 2 of the ESM Treaty are incompatible with Article 125 TFEU in that they imply that the ESM Members guarantee the debt of the defaulting member.

According to Article 25 para 2 of the ESM Treaty, if an ESM Member fails to meet the required payment under a capital call, a revised increased capital call shall be made to all ESM Members with a view to ensuring that the ESM receives the total amount of paid-in capital needed. The same provision provides that the Board of Governors shall decide an appropriate course of action for ensuring that the ESM Member concerned settles its debt to the ESM within a reasonable period of time and shall be entitled to require the payment of default interest on the overdue amount.

It results expressly from this provision, as results also from the Court's judgment, that in the framework of the capital calls procedure provided for in Article 25 para 2 of the ESM Treaty, the ESM Member States do not act as guarantors for the defaulting ESM Member State.

In this context, the Court concludes that Article 125 TFEU does not preclude the conclusion and the ratification of the ESM Treaty by the Member States whose currency is the Euro. The leit motif in this part of the judgment is that, by intervening, the ESM does not take charge of the obligation of the debtor Member State.

The efforts of the Court to develop, for the first time, a structured reasoning on the no bail-out clause must be welcomed. The Court did not take position on all the arguments developed before it, but in a synthetic way tried to lay the basis of the new legal doctrine according to which Member State assistance to other Member States is compatible with the no bail-out clause.

However, the fact that the Court did not clearly reject the arguments formulated by many authors concerning the scope of Article 125 TFEU has been considered as a kind of an admission that there are instruments of financial assistance such as the instruments adopted during the crisis the last three years (in particular the EFSF and the Greek loan), which are no compatible with Article 125 TFEU. In this context, one could argue that the reservations of the national courts concerning the scope of this provision, such as exposed by the BVG in its latest judgment regarding the ESM and the STACOG, are still relevant. Therefore, even after the judgment of the Court in the Pringle case, the doctrinal debate on the scope of the no bail-out clause seems not to be closed.[16]

We do not share this point of view. The Court took a very lucid position concerning the scope of Article 125 TFEU and closed the lasting academic debate of the last three years. Probably, the Court could have addressed all the argumentation developed in relation to the scope of Article 125 TFEU. However, given the nature of the litigation, and its high political sensitivity, the Court decided to go straight to the point and not to further prolong its reasoning which, compared to its standard case law relating to the preliminary ruling procedures, is already rather long.

[16] See inter alia Calliess (2013), pp. 97–105, sp. 103; Frenz (2013), pp. 27–32, sp. 30 and 32; Glaser (2013), pp. 167–169, sp. 168; Vogel (2013), pp. 45–46.

In addition, it must be observed that, without prejudice to the primacy of the judgments of the Court vis-à-vis those of the national courts, there is a general feeling that a permanent dialogue must be established between the supreme courts of the Member States and the CJEU.[17] This is particularly true when the views of these courts do not coincide differs from that of the national courts. Again, we do not share this point of view. Aside from the political issue at the basis of this argument, there is no legal ground on which this argument can be based.

4.3 The Conclusion of the ESM Treaty and the Role Allocated by This Treaty to the EU Institutions (Article 13 TEU)

It must be reminded that the ESM Treaty has been concluded exclusively by Member States and not by the EU, and that the Court recognized its jurisdiction to interpret this agreement in the particular context of a reference for a preliminary ruling. In this context, as mentioned above, the Court developed for the first time a very structured interpretation of the main provisions of the economic pillar of the EU. However, at the same time, the peculiar nature of its review allowed the Court to take some new positions. This was more obvious where the Court examined in its judgment the compatibility of the ESM Treaty with Article 13 TEU for the reason that the ESM Treaty allocated an important role to the EU institutions.

In particular, the referring judge asked the Court whether the allocation by the ESM Treaty of new tasks to the Commission, the ECB and the Court itself is compatible with their powers as defined in the Treaties. One should observe that, although the ESM Treaty involved the main EU institutions, the contracting parties remarkably decided that the European Parliament would not be involved.

Given the difference of the functions of the three mentioned EU institutions in the ESM Treaty framework, the Court examined on the one hand the role allocated to the ECB and the Commission (Sect. 4.3.1) and, on the other hand, the role of the Court itself (Sect. 4.3.2).

4.3.1 The Conclusion of the ESM Treaty and the Role Allocated to the Commission and the ECB in the ESM Framework

It results expressly from the ESM Treaty that, in the framework put in place by the ESM, the Commission and the ECB are assigned an active role and specific tasks.

[17] Schunder (2013), p. 1.

Firstly, the authors of the ESM Treaty provided that the Commission and the ECB can be involved jointly in the governance framework of this Treaty. For instance:

- When the Commission and the ECB conclude that a failure to urgently adopt a decision to grant or implement financial assistance would threaten the economic and financial sustainability of the euro area, an emergency voting procedure shall be used pursuant to Article 4 para 4 of the ESM Treaty.
- The members of the European Commission in charge of the economic and monetary affairs and the President of the ECB may participate as observers in the meetings of the Board of Governors (Article 5 para 3) and the Board of Directors (Article 6 para 2).
- The European Commission could receive, in liaison with the ECB, a mandate from the Board of Governors to negotiate the economic policy conditionality attached to each financial assistance (Article 5 para 6(g).
- Concerning, in particular, the procedure to grant stability support (Article 13 para 1), the chairperson of the Board of Governors shall entrust the Commission, in liaison with the ECB, with the task to assess, firstly, the existence of a risk to the financial stability of the Euro area as a whole, secondly, whether public debt is sustainable and, thirdly, to assess the actual or potential financing means of the ESM Member concerned.
- When the Board of Governors decides to grant stability support to an ESM Member, in the form of a financial assistance facility, the Board shall entrust the Commission, in liaison with the ECB, with the task to negotiate with the ESM Member concerned a Memorandum of Understanding detailing the conditionality attached to the financial assistance facility (Article 13 para 3). In the same context, the European Commission, in liaison with the ECB, shall be entrusted with monitoring compliance with the conditionality attached to this assistance (Article 13 para 7).
- The Board of Directors shall decide, by mutual agreement on a proposal from the Managing Director and based on an assessment by the Commission and the ECB, whether the credit line continues to be adequate or whether another form of financial assistance is needed (Article 14 para 6).

Secondly, the authors of the ESM Treaty conferred a specific role on the European Commission alone. For instance, in the procedure to grant stability support, it is the Commission that signs the Memorandum of Understanding on behalf of the ECB (Article 13 para 4). Concerning a precautionary conditioned credit line, the Board of Directors shall decide, by mutual agreement, on a proposal from the Managing Director, and after having received a report from the European Commission, whether the credit line should be maintained (Article 14 para 5). Article 15 para 5 (recapitalization of financial institutions of an ESM Members), 16 para 5 (ESM loans), 17 para 5 (primary market support facilities) all provide, inter alia, that the Board of Directors decides after having received a report of the European Commission on the disbursement of the financial assistance or of the tranches of the financial assistance to a beneficiary Member State.

Thirdly, the authors of the ESM Treaty conferred a specific role on the ECB in the framework of the secondary market support facility. Indeed, according to Article 18 para 2, decisions on intervention on the secondary markets to address contagion shall be taken on the basis of an analysis of the ECB recognizing the existence of exceptional financial market circumstances and risks to financial stability.

The authors of this Treaty conferred diverse tasks and roles to the ECB and the European Commission. However, the action of the two EU institutions is limited to the internal functioning of the legal framework of the ESM and does not encroach upon the competence of these institutions, such as provided for in the EU Treaties. In particular, the Commission and the ECB have no decisional powers in the framework of the ESM Treaty in relation to the TFEU and, in any case, their actions do not bind the EU. The authors of the ESM Treaty intended to confer on the involved EU institutions in principle a kind of managing role, as results in particular from Article 13 of this Treaty.

Nevertheless, the Court stated that *"it is apparent from the case-law of the Court that the Member States are entitled, in areas which do not fall under the exclusive competence of the Union, to entrust tasks to the institutions, outside the framework of the Union, such as the task of coordinating a collective action undertaken by the Member States or managing financial assistance, provided that those tasks do not alter the essential character of the powers conferred on those institutions by the EU and FEU Treaties"* (para 158).

In order to justify its statement, the Court recalls its case law concerning the areas which do not fall under the exclusive competence of the EU. This case law was established by the Court in the field of the EU external relations and, in particular, for international agreements in which the European Union (European Communities) was a contracting party or for litigations whose main issue was precisely the nature (exclusive or shared) of the competence of the European Union to participate to and conclude the relevant agreement. This is, however, not the case in the current litigation.

The Court repeats many times in its judgment that the European Union does not have a specific competence to act in the field of financial assistance, such as determined by the ESM Treaty and, in any case, the amendment of Article 136 TFEU confirms the competence of the Member States. In its judgment, the Court does not qualify the competence in the field of the financial assistance envisaged by the ESM as *"shared"* between the EU and its Member States. Nevertheless, following the reasoning of the Court, this competence is to be considered as mixed.

The Court concluded that the duties conferred on the Commission and ECB within the ESM Treaty, important as they are, do not entail any power to make decisions of their own. Furthermore, the activities pursued by those two institutions within the ESM Treaty solely commit the ESM (para 161).

The Court could have finished its statement in this paragraph, but by referring to its case law preferred to specify that the tasks conferred on the Commission and the ECB do not alter the essential character of the powers conferred on those institutions by the EU and FEU Treaties (para 162). This is the new element in the case law of the Court.

As regards the Commission, the Court observed that Article 17 para 1 TEU provides that the Commission" *shall promote the general interest of the Union*" and" *shall oversee the application of Union law*". The Court added that the objective of the ESM Treaty is to ensure the financial stability of the euro area as a whole. By its involvement in the ESM Treaty, the Commission promotes the general interest of the Union. Furthermore, the tasks allocated to the Commission by the ESM Treaty enable it, as provided in Article 13(3) and (4) of that treaty, to ensure that the memoranda of understanding concluded by the ESM are consistent with European Union law (para 163–164).

The involvement of the European Commission in an international agreement concluded exclusively by the Member States, such as the ESM Treaty, had the purpose to influence the development of the ESM framework from a European Union law standpoint. The actions undertaken by this European institution in this framework could be considered in the middle run as the basis on which a kind of *acquis* in the field of financial assistance law could be developed in the future.

It is true that the ESM Treaty does not provide for an express procedure in this respect, although the STACOG Treaty—also an agreement concluded exclusively by the Member States—does provide for this possibility (Article 16). Indeed, according to this provision, *"Within five years at most following the entry into force of this Treaty, on the basis of an assessment of the experience with its implementation, the necessary steps shall be taken, in compliance with the provisions of the Treaty on the European Union and the Treaty on the Functioning of the European Union, with the aim of incorporating the substance of this Treaty into the legal framework of the European Union"*. However, the Pringle judgment makes up for the lack of such a provision in the ESM. In this perspective, it is to be welcomed.

As regards the tasks allocated to the ECB by the ESM Treaty, the Court observed that they are in line with the various tasks which the TFEU and the Statute of the ESCB confer on that institution and that the ECB supports the general economic policies in the Union, in accordance with Article 282 para 2 TFEU (para 165).

The tasks conferred on the ECB have a different profile than those conferred on the European Commission. The Court pointed out the peculiarity of these tasks and stressed that, in any case, the participation of the ECB in the ESM framework is in line with the Statute of the ESCB because Article 6 para 2 of the Statute provides that the ECB is entitled to participate in international monetary institutions. Article 23 of that Statute confirms also that the ECB may *"establish relations ... with organizations"* (para 166). For the Court, the ESM Treaty is an economic forum very close to a separate international organization. This is a new element in the case law of the Court of Justice.

Finally, the Court examined if the involvement of the Commission and the ECB in the ESM Treaty framework can infringe, in general, the regime of enhanced cooperation provided for in Article 20 para 1 TEU. The Court observed that, according to this provision, enhanced cooperation may be established only where the Union itself is competent to act in the area concerned by that cooperation. However, for the Court, the EU Treaties do not confer on the Union a specific competence to establish a permanent stability mechanism such as the ESM (paras 167–168).

The argument on enhanced cooperation is examined by the Court incidentally. However, the issue of the enhanced cooperation in this field is very important because the ESM Treaty was concluded only by the EU Member States whose currency is the euro. Indeed, one of the main issues of the enhanced cooperation is also whether the Member States could put in place and complete such cooperation via an international agreement. The Court preferred to avoid any comments on this issue, and based its reasoning on the fact that the enhanced cooperation may be established only where the Union itself is competent to act in the area concerned by that cooperation.

It is true that one of the main conclusions of the Court in the Pringle judgment is that the Union has no specific competence to establish the ESM. However, as mentioned above, in our view this conclusion should have preferably been nuanced. Indeed, the fact that the EU has no competence to establish a stability mechanism does not mean that the European Union has not a residual competence in the field of financial assistance. The Court itself recognized in the Pringle judgment the existence of such competence for the temporary financial assistance measures in relation to Article 122 para 2 TFEU.

It is in those circumstances that the Court concluded that Article 20 TEU does not preclude the conclusion or the ratification by the Member States whose currency is the euro of an agreement such as the ESM Treaty.

4.3.2 The Conclusion of the ESM Treaty and the Role Allocated to the Court

Under Article 37 para 2 of the ESM Treaty, the Board of Governors decides on any dispute arising between an ESM Member and the ESM, or between ESM Members, in connection with the interpretation and application of the ESM Treaty, including any dispute about the compatibility of the decisions adopted by the ESM with that treaty. According to Article 37 para 3 of this treaty, ESM Members can challenge the decision referred to in para 2 before the Court of Justice. The judgment of the Court shall be binding on the parties in the procedure, which must take the necessary measures to comply with the judgment within a period to be decided by the said Court. In addition, it results from recital 16 of the preamble to the ESM Treaty that the Court's jurisdiction under Article 37 para 3 of the ESM Treaty is conferred on the basis of Article 273 TFEU.

In this framework the question is whether this jurisdiction is compatible with the role and the powers that the European Treaties confer to the Court. Since its well known Opinion 1/91 (mentioned above), the Court established an important legal doctrine under which the Member States cannot conclude an international agreement when such agreement could affect the role and the jurisdiction of the European Court as determined in the European Treaties. In this respect, the Court developed the notion of the *"foundations of the Community legal order"* and concluded that an agreement which could infringe the fundamental role of the Court such as determined in the former Article 164 of the TEEC must be declared incompatible with EU law.

However, as we mentioned above, this case law of the Court is not automatically applicable in the current litigation. Firstly, the European Union is not a contracting party of the ESM Treaty and secondly the Court of Justice of the European Union does not exercise its powers under the general Treaty provisions on the Court's jurisdiction, but rather on the basis of the special regime contained in Article 273 TFEU. In this respect, the Court should only assess whether the conditions laid down by this Article are respected by the wording and purpose of Article 37 of the ESM Treaty.

Under Article 273 TFEU the *"The Court of Justice shall have jurisdiction in any dispute between Member States which relate to the subject matter of the Treaty if the dispute is submitted to it under a special agreement between the parties"*. The French version of this provision refers to disputes *"en connexité avec l'objet des traités"*. A first comparison of the two versions leads to conclude that there is a substantial difference about the domains of the disputes which are subject to the jurisdiction of the Court. In this respect, the Court could have perhaps clarified the meaning of the French wording *"litiges en connexité avec l'objet des traités"*.

As a preliminary remark, it must be considered that Article 273 TFEU contains a kind of arbitration clause for the Court of Justice concerning in particular certain disputes between the Member States. The context of the jurisdiction of the Court on the basis of this article is different from that of the jurisdiction conferred on the basis of Article 272 TFEU. The latter refers to an arbitration clause contained in a contract (governed by public or private law) concluded by or on behalf of the Union. A significant case law was developed on the basis of this provision by the General Court and the Court of Justice of the European Union.[18] In contrast, the Court never had the occasion to interpret Article 273 TFEU.

On the basis of Article 273 TFEU, three main conditions must be examined. Firstly, the existence of a special agreement conferring jurisdiction to the Court. Secondly, that this jurisdiction is related to the subject matter of the Treaties (*"litiges en connexité avec l'objet des traités"*); thirdly, the existence of a dispute between Member States.

---

[18] See inter alia Case T-259/09, *Commission v/Arci Nuova associazione comitato di Cagliari et Gessa,* [2010] ECR II-284 and Case T-460/08, *Commission v/Acentro Turismo,* [2010] ECR II-6351; Case C-623/11, *Geodis Calberson GE,* Judgment of the Court of 17 January 2013, nyr and Case C-314/11P, *European Commission v Planet AE,* Judgment of the Court of 19 December 2012, nyr.

According to the Court the first condition is fulfilled, because *"there is no reason, given the objective pursued by that provision, why such agreement should not be given in advance, with reference to a whole class of pre-defined disputes, by means of a provision such as Article 37(3) of the ESM Treaty"* (para 172).

This interpretation of the Court is very pragmatic: Article 273 TFEU requires a special agreement but indeed the Member States could incorporate this special agreement in the full text of the agreement for which the arbitration of the Court is requested. The wording used in the ESM Treaty and its recital 16 does not provide for the necessity to adopt a separate agreement conferring jurisdiction to the Court. However, the Court reconciles this inconsistency and its reasoning must therefore be welcomed.

It must be reminded that in this respect the ESM Treaty differs from the STACOG Treaty. Indeed, the latter provides for an explicit formulation of the arbitration clause concerning the jurisdiction of the Court of Justice. Under Article 8 para 3 of the STACOG Treaty, *"this Article (Article 8 para 3) constitutes a special agreement between the Contracting Parties within the meaning of Article 273 of the Treaty on the Functioning of the European Union"*. Article 8 para 1 and 8 para 2 of the STACOG Treaty provide for a special infringement procedure with a limited scope against the Member States which fail to respect their obligations under the STACOG Treaty. Paragraph 3 of the same Article expressly mentions that Member States accept on the basis of a special agreement the jurisdiction of the Court.[19]

In contrast to the ESM and to the STACOG Treaty, Article 16 para 2 of the EFSF framework agreement provides that in the absence of an amicable agreement in case of a dispute between EFSF contracting Member States only, such dispute shall be submitted to the exclusive jurisdiction of the Court of Justice of the European Union without mention to Article 273 TFEU and also to any special agreement comparable to the STACOG Treaty. There is no doubt however that the above disputes can only be brought before the Court on the basis of Article 273 TFEU. Indeed, the EFSF Framework Agreement concluded between the EFSF and the seventeen Member State of the euro area could no fall within the scope of Article 272 TFEU.

The difference of the STACOG Treaty vis-à-vis the ESM Treaty and the EFSF Framework Agreement lies in that it mentions the existence of a special agreement conferring jurisdiction to the Court for the STACOG Treaty itself.

Secondly, concerning the condition according to which the disputes to be submitted to the jurisdiction of the Court must be related to the subject-matter of the Treaties, the Court considered that a dispute linked to the interpretation or application of the ESM Treaty is also likely to concern the interpretation or application of provisions of European Union law. Under Article 13(3) of the ESM Treaty, the MoU which is to be negotiated with the Member State requesting stability support must be fully consistent with European Union law and, in particular, with the measures taken by the Union in the area of coordination of the economic policies of the Member States. Accordingly, the conditions to be attached to the grant

[19] See Louis (2013), pp. 5–22, sp. 15.

of such support to a Member State are, at least in part, determined by European Union law (para 174).

The English wording used by this provision, *"dispute relating to subject matter of the treaty"*, is clearer than the French version *"litiges en connexité avec l'objet des Traités"*. The Court did not remark this language difference and instead preferred not to point out the relevant criteria according to which a dispute could be considered as related to the subject matter dispute or *"en connexité avec l'objet des Traités"*. The Court mentioned in a general way that a dispute linked to the interpretation or application of the ESM Treaty is likely to concern also the interpretation or application of provisions of EU law.

One could consider that with this wording, *"en connexité avec l'objet des Traités"*, the authors of the Treaty envisaged to confer on the Court a jurisdiction for disputes which are not covered by the general jurisdiction of the Court. In contrast, if the Court had jurisdiction to solve disputes between Member States directly in the field of EU Treaties, the regime of the infringement procedure provided by the Treaties (Article 258 TFEU) would be circumvented. In any case, in order for this *"connexité"* to be established, the dispute of the Member States must be related to the *"objet des Traités"*. This wording could be interpreted in an extremely extensive way. It must also be observed that a similar wording is used in the former Article 235 of the Treaty establishing the European Economic Community, then become Article 308 TEC, now Article 352 TFEU, which mentions *"les objectifs visés par le Traité"*. This kind of wording allows a broad interpretation of the relevant provisions.

The efforts to interpret this provision could highlight doubts as for the real meaning of this provision. As an arbitration clause, Article 273 TFEU must concern a priori issues between the Member States which do not fall within the general jurisdiction of the Court such as determined by the relevant provision of EU law.

Article 273 TFEU probably expresses the idea that in any case, disputes between Member States should be settled before the Court of Justice rather than other alternative dispute settlement fora. Certainly, the Treaties recognize the right to confer jurisdiction to the Court under Article 273 TFEU as an option for the Member States (necessity of a specific agreement) and not as an obligation. However, for the authors of the Treaties the Court must be considered as the ultimate judge and in any case the last suitable arbiter of a dispute between Member States in order to protect in a more general perspective the cohesion and the *"unity"*[20] of EU law.

Thirdly, concerning the existence of a dispute between Member States, the Court recognized that *"it is true that the jurisdiction of the Court under Article 273 TFEU is subject to the condition that only Members States are parties to the dispute submitted to it"* (para 175). According to Article 37 of the ESM Treaty, the dispute could arise between ESM Member States but also between ESM Member States and the ESM as an independent entity. In the latter case, the dispute is not formally between Member States.

---

[20] See Craig (2012), pp. 231–248, sp. 245.

In this respect, however, the Court answered generally without precision that "*since the membership of the ESM consists solely of Member States, a dispute to which the ESM is party may be considered to be a dispute between Member States within the meaning of Article 273 TFEU*". This is a new element of the case law of the Court and the following observations must be made. The Court seems to state that the ESM—despite its own system of governance—is not considered as a structure independent from its Member States.

However, in paras 165–167 of the judgment and in order to justify the specific rules on the ECB, the Court took a different position indicating that Article 6 para 2 of the Statute provides that the ECB is entitled to participate in international monetary institutions and Article 23 of that Statute provides that the ECB may "*establish relations ... with organizations*" (para 166). In this part of the judgment, the Court seems to recognize that the ESM has a specific and independent structure from its Member States which also could be present in the international arena. In addition it is generally admitted that the ESM constitutes a new international organization independent from its Member States.[21] From a combined reading, the two parts of the judgment could appear partly conflicting.

The interpretation of the Court regarding the last condition of Article 273 TFEU (dispute between Member States) is a new element in the case law of the European Court of Justice which, however, would need further consolidation in the future.

In addition, it must be stated that the interpretation of the Court on the ESM Treaty is not ipso facto applicable to the STACOG Treaty and to the EFSF Framework Agreement. Indeed, in these two Treaties, the Court has jurisdiction only on cases concerning exclusively Member States between themselves. In addition, it must be observed that the EFSM Framework Agreement and the STACOG Treaty, in contrast with the ESM, do not put in place an independent and autonomous organization having its own governance system.

Under that condition, the Court concludes that the allocation to the Court, of the jurisdiction to interpret and apply the provisions of that treaty (Article 37(3) of the ESM Treaty) satisfies the conditions laid down in Article 273 TFEU and more generally that Article 13 TEU does not preclude the conclusion by the Member States whose currency is the euro of an agreement such as the ESM Treaty.

4.4 The ESM Treaty and the Charter

The CJEU was invited to answer to the question whether the consequence of establishing the ESM outside the European Union legal order can be that the ESM is removed from the scope of the Charter, thus breaching the right to effective judicial protection granted by Article 47.

By referring to Article 51 para 1 of the Charter, the Court observed that "*its provisions are addressed to the Member States only when they are implementing*

[21] See Ruffert (2011), pp. 1777–1806, sp. 1783 and Jansen (2011), pp. 417–423, sp. 418.

Union law" and that *"under Article 51 para 2, the Charter does not extend the field of application of Union law beyond the powers of the Union, or establish any new power or task for the Union or modify powers and tasks as defined in the Treaties". "Accordingly, the Court is called upon to interpret, in the light of the Charter, the law of the European Union within the limits of the powers conferred on it"* (para 179).

From the above provision, the Court concludes that the Member States are not implementing Union law within the meaning of this article when they establish a stability mechanism such as the ESM, where the EU and FEU Treaties do not confer any specific competence on the Union to establish such a mechanism. In those conditions, the Court stated that the general principle of effective judicial protection does not preclude the conclusion by the Member States whose currency is the euro of an agreement such as the ESM Treaty.

Although this conclusion is formally correct, one should ask the question whether the Court needed to take this position precisely such as developed before the Court by the parties. The Court did not have the necessary elements to give its answer and, in any case, the fact that the applicant (Mr Pringle) in the national proceeding was able to bring the action before the national court and to challenge the validity of European Council Decision 2011/199 is evidence that the principle of right to an effective judicial protection is effectively guaranteed.

In any case, the position of the Court needs to be discussed as follows. The Court based its reasoning on the fact that the establishment of the ESM Treaty outside the European Union legal order avoids breaching the right to effective jurisdictional protection by reference to Article 51 of the Charter. Indeed this Article provides expressly that the provisions of the Charter are addressed to Member States only when these are implementing EU law. The ESM Treaty is not considered as EU law.

However, the right to an effective judicial protection as a fundamental principle has its source not only in the Charter. The Court preferred to ground its reasoning on the formal rule contained in Article 51 of the Charter without nevertheless giving a clear answer if the right to an effective judicial protection as a general principle is effectively ensured by the Member States. Before the Court of Justice it is supported expressly that the applicant was able to bring an action before the national court and to fully contest the validity European Council Decision 2011/199. The Court failed to point out that in any case, in the Pringle litigation the right to an effective judicial protection is respected.

4.5 Conclusion

One of the most significant innovations brought about by the Pringle judgment is the examination in the framework of a reference for a preliminary ruling of the compatibilty with EU primary law of an international agreement concluded exclusively by the Member States, such as the ESM.

The Court made a substantial effort to recognize that the ESM Treaty is in line with all the relevant provisions of EU primary law.[22] The Court followed a pragmatic approach in order to safeguard the validity of ESM Treaty. In certain instances such as in relation to Article 122 para 2 TFEU, the enhanced cooperation regime and the interpretation of Article 273 TFEU, the Court has privileged a formal interpretation concluding that the ESM is compatible with the Treaties. In addition, the Court made numerous references to its case law, although in some instances the pertinence of such references might be questioned, considering the completely new issues discussed in the Pringle judgment.

One could argue that this approach of the Court was preferable than one liable to reveal some inconsistencies of the ESM with the EU legal framework and therefore provoke negative consequences on the ESM and more generally the Euro area. However, from a strictly legal perspective, this aim of the Court goes beyond its formal mandate. For instance, following its previous case law, the Court could have concluded that it has no jurisdiction in order to interpret agreements entered into exclusively by Member States. The Court, instead, recognized its jurisdiction and thus showed its interest to participate to the elaboration of the new European law which has developed in the past five years in the absence of an adequate EU framework.

From a reading of the Pringle judgment as a whole, one clearly perceives the Court's effort to demonstrate that the framework of the Economic and Monetary Union should coexist with the ESM framework. In addition, and after having explained why this coexistence must be accepted, the Court also supported the view that the establishment of the ESM Treaty does not infringe the institutional framework of the EU. In this respect, three additional comments must be made.

Firstly, regarding the monetary pillar of the EMU, the Court had to demonstrate why the financial assistance put in place with the ESM Treaty does not infringe the monetary policy. In order to avoid any contradiction between the stability mechanism and the monetary pillar of the EMU, the Court based its reasoning on a new concept that is the safeguard of the *"stability of the euro area as a whole"*. The Court did not find any objection to use this concept in order to justify its statements. The Court also developed an important reasoning on the potential influence of the activities of the ESM on the inflation rate and on other economic indicators. Being very ambitious in explaining this position, the Court had to take some risks developing an economic reasoning.

The Court's analysis of the exclusive nature of monetary policy is also combined with its analysis of the rules on the exercise of the exclusive competences. In this respect, the Court developed a detailed analysis on the possibility that the conclusion of the ESM Treaty affects common EU rules or alters their scope. The Court focused on the first hypothesis, that is to say the non-affectation of the common rules. For this reason, its statements are not always strong, for instance those on the impact of the ESM Treaty on the EFSM and in general on the framework which could be put in place under Article 122 para 2 TFEU.

[22] See Picod (2012), pp. 2260 and Thomas (2013), pp. 198–206, sp. 206.

Secondly, concerning the economic pillar of the EMU, it is important to point out that, for the first time, the Court developed an exhaustive analysis of Articles 122 TFEU, 123 TFEU and 125 TFEU. Concerning Article 122 TFEU and the ad hoc financial assistance provided for by this provision, we can observe the Court's uneasiness when it came to combine the framework envisaged by this provision and the financial assistance framework established by the ESM Treaty. Concerning the monetary financing prohibition, the Court solidly demonstrates that this prohibition, which is addressed to the central banks, does not apply to the Member States, and therefore cannot be invoked in the framework of the ESM Treaty. The Court's interpretation of the no bail-out clause (Article 125 TFEU) constitutes, on the other hand, one of the most significant statements in this judgment. The Court recognizes that the prohibition contained in this clause is not absolute and, through a very structured reasoning, concludes that this clause does not represent an obstacle to the implementation of the ESM Treaty.

However, one might regret the Court's wish to develop a certain economic reasoning regarding the impact of the support measures in the primary and secondary market, and more generally its wish to develop, via a judicial technique, an economic reasoning whose solidity is not certain. In any case, with its statements on Articles 122, 123 and 125 TFEU the Court reminded to the national judges its privilege to interpreter the primary Union law, in particular when the "acte clair" theory could be considered as the pretext in order not to refer to the Court.[23]

It is also interesting to observe the analysis of the Court regarding the impact of the ESM Treaty on the general legal framework of the EU. While it is true that, regarding the monetary and economic pillar of the EMU, the Court tried to demonstrate a certain innovation with the elaboration of some new concepts, the same conclusion cannot be reached with regard to the institutional framework of the EU. For instance, the analysis of the Court regarding the enhanced cooperation is minimalistic. The same conclusion can be reached regarding in particular the interpretation of Article 273 TFEU. We observe the difficulty of the Court to analyze what really means a dispute with the ESM in *"connexité avec l'objet du Traité"*. Indeed, despite the effort of the Court to recognize that in any case the ESM framework must coexist with the EMU and the EU, in its analysis of Article 273 TFEU, the Court pointed out that disputes between the ESM and Member States must be considered as comparable to disputes between Member States such as provided in the ESM Treaty.

The Court seems to consider that the ESM is not independent from its Member States, although this Treaty contains important provisions regarding its own system of governance (board of governors, board of directors etc.). In this respect also, it must be reminded that the board of governors is allowed to amend certain provisions of the ESM Treaty (e.g. capital stock, maximum landing volume, type of instruments of financial assistance) (Articles 10 and 19 ESM). It seems excessively formal to consider that *since the membership of the ESM consists solely of*

[23] See in a different context about the role of the CJEU Pernice (2011), pp. 151–168, sp. 165.

Member States, a dispute to which the ESM is party may be considered to be a dispute between Member States within the meaning of Article 273 TFEU. In the future, a clarification of this point will be useful.

Finally, concerning the possible breach of the Charter resulting from the fact that the ESM was concluded outside the EU legal order, the Court has adopted a formal reasoning on the basis of Article 51 of the Charter, although it had the possibility to demonstrate that such violation could not be established.

References

Allemand F, Martucci F (2012) La nouvelle Gouvernance économique européenne II. CDE 409–457

Ahari A. (2012) Der ESM und die Verfassung—Erste Gedanken zur Entscheidung des Deutschen Bundesverfassungsgercht vom 12.9.2012. ÖJZ:878–880

Allemand F. (2012) La faisabilité juridique des projets d'euro-obligations RTDE 553–594

Calliess C. (2013) Der ESM zwischen Luxemburg und Karlsruhe—Die Krise der Währungsunion als Bewährungsprobe der Rechtsgemeinschaft. NVwZ 97–105

Cecchini G.L. (2012), BCE e ESM (European stability mechanism) : quale sovranità per lo Stato? RCGI 122–131

Craig P (2012) The Stability, Coordination and governance treaty: principle, politics and pragmatism ELR 231–248

de Gregorio Merino A, (2012) Legal Developments in the Economic and Monetary Union during the debt crisis: the mechanism of financial assistance, CMLRev 1613–1646

Dechâtre L (2011) La décision de Karlsruhe sur le mécanisme de stabilité financière: une validité sous conditions et une mise en garde sibylline pour l'avenir. CDE 2011 303–342

Dehousse F (1995) Commentaire de l'Article 104 B TCE, In: Constantinesco, Kovar, Simon (eds) Traité sur l'Union européenne (signé à Maastricht le 7 février 1992) Commentaire article par article, Economica, Paris

Frenz, W (2013) ESM-Vertrag europarechtskonform!? EWS 27–32

Gautier Y (2004) La competence communuatire exclusive. In : Mélanges en hommage à Guy Isaac. 50 ans de droit communautaire. Tome 2, Presses de l'Université des sciences sociales, Toulouse, pp 165–189

Glaser A (2013) Zur Gültigkeit des Euro-Stabilitätsmechanismus (ESM-Vertrag). DVBl 167–169

Häde U (2009) Haushaltdisziplin und Solidarität im Zeichen des Finankrise. EuZW 399–403

Hentschelmann K (2011) Finanzhilfen im Lichte der No Bailout Klausel—Eigenverantwortung und Solidarität in der Währungsunion. EuR 282–312

Herrmann C (2010) Griechische Tragödie – der währungsverfassungsrechtiliche Rahmen für die Rettung, den Austritt oder den Ausschluss von überschuldeten Staaten aus der Eurozone. EuZW 413–416

Jansen R (2011) The European financial stability facility (EFSF) and the European stability mechanism (ESM). Euredia 417–423

Louis J-V (2004) Monnaie (Union Economique et Monétaire), Rép. Communautaire Dalloz, Mis à jour 2012

Louis J-V (2009) L'Union européenne et sa monnaie. Commentaire Mégret 3ème Edition. Editions de l'Université de Bruxelles—IEE, Bruxelles

Louis J-V (2010) Editorial Comments, The no-bailout clause and rescue packages. CMLRev 971–986

Louis J-V (2013) Un traité vite fait bien fait?, Le traité du 2 mars 2012 sur la stabilité la coordination et la gouvernance au sein de l'Union économique et monétaire RTDE 5–22

Martucci F (2010) Commentaire de l'Article 103 TCE. In: Commentaire Article par article des traités UE et CE, De Rome à Lisbonne (Pingel eds), Helbing Lichtenhahn Dalloz and Bruylant, Basel, Paris, Brussel

Mayer C (2012) Vertrag über Stabilität, Koordinierung und Steuerung in der WWU und Europäischer Stabilit!atsmechanismus. JRP 124–136

Middleton T (2012) Not bailing out … legal aspect of the Sovereign debt crisis. In: Liber Amicorum en l'honneur de Jean-Claude Piris: a man for all treaties. Bruylant, Bruxelles, pp 422–425

Palmostorfer R (2012) To bail out or not bail out? The current framework of financial assistance for euro area member States measured against the requirements of the EU primary law. ELR 771–784

Pernice I (2011) Die Zukunft der Unionsgerichtsbarkeit. Zu den Bedingungen einer nachhaltigen Sicherung effektiven Rechtsschutzes im Europäischen Verfassungsverbund. Eur 151–168

Picod F (2012) Rien ne s'oppose au traité instituant le mécanisme européen de stabilité. JCP 50:2260

Ruffert M (2011) The European debt crisis and European Union law. CMLRev 1777–1806

Santulli C (2011) L'Euro : analyse juridique de la « crise de la dette. RGDIP 833–851

Schneider K (2013) Yes, but … one more thing: Karlsruhe's ruling on the European stability mechanism. GLJ 53–74

Schunder A (2013) Editorial. Rettungsschirm gerettet! NVwZ 1

Seidel M (2011) Gastkommentar. Die no-bail-out-klausel des Article. AEUV als Beistandsverbot. EuZWR 125:529–530

Sester P (2011) Beteiligung von privaten Investoren an der Umschuldung von Staatsanleihen im Rahmen des Europe an Stability Mechanism (ESM). ZWBR 1057–1066

Sester P (2012a) Die Role der EZB in der europäischen Staatsschuldenkrise. EWS 80–90

Sester P (2012b) The ECB's Controversial Securities Market Programme (SMP) and its role in relation to the modified EFSF and the future ESM. ECFLR:156-178

Thomas S (2013) La jurisprudence de la Cour de justice et du Tribunal de l'Union européenne. Chronique des arrêts. Arrêt « Pringle ». RDUE 198–206

Tomkin J (2013) Contradiction, Circumvention and Conceptual Gymnasticks: The Impact of the Adoption of the ESM Treaty on the State of the European Democracy. GLJ 169–189

Tomuschat C (2012) Anmerkung zum Urteil des BVerfG vom 12.09.2012—BvR 1390/122—u.a. Verhinderung der ratification von ESM—Vertrag und Fiscalpakt überwiegend erfolgos. DVBl 1431–1434

Vogel M (2013) Rechtsprechung der EU-Gerichte. Kommentar. EWS 45–46

Wendel M (2013) Judicial restraint and the return to openness: the decision of the German Federal Constitutional Court on the ESM and the Fiscal Treaty of 12 September 2012. GLJ 21–52

Chapter 5
The Pringle Judgment and Future Perspectives

As a first remark, the Court widened the scope of its jurisdiction in order to interpret an international agreement concluded exclusively by Member States. In this type of instruments, the Court sees very important implications to the EU legal order and it therefore considered that even in the absence of any EU law provision conferring Juridiction to the Court in that particular context, the latter must remain the sole judge in order to solve dispute between Member States.

This position is very important because in order to face the crisis the Member States decided to act via the conclusion of international agreements such as the ESM, the STACOG Treaty and the EFSF Framework Agreement. It is not excluded that in the future, the Member States will adopt other international agreements in order to develop the EU law-related issues, in particular in the framework of the European Monetary Union which, by its constitution, presents a very important institutional differentiation with the European Union as whole.

It must be reminded that in the past, the Treaty of Rome provided for, in particular, the possibility for the Member States to adopt international agreements to develop into the EC legal order some specific areas of intervention. Indeed, former Article 220 of the EEC Treaty provided that Member States would, so far as necessary, enter into negotiations with each other with a view to securing for the benefit of their nationals the establishment of rules intended to facilitate the achievement of the common market in the various spheres listed in that provision. In this line, for instance, the Convention of 27 September 1968 on Jurisdiction and Enforcement of Judgments in Civil and Commercial Matters was adopted. This Convention was established on the basis of the mentioned above Article 220. From this point of view, since the establishment of the European Communities, the European primary law did not exclude the possibility for the Member States to establish cooperation frameworks into the European legal order and some authors have qualified this source as *sources complémentaires*[1] of community law.

---

[1] See for instance Isaac (1992), p 136.

E. de Lhoneux and C. A. Vassilopoulos, *The European Stability Mechanism Before the Court of Justice of the European Union*, SpringerBriefs in Law,
DOI: 10.1007/978-3-319-01478-4_5,

The Member States developed this cooperation also in other specific and sensitive matters with the adoption, inter alia, of the Schengen Treaty and the Prüm Treaty (called Schengen III[2]) in the field of the free movement and the common market. However, this cooperation is different from the cooperation established in the field of the economic pillar of the EMU with the conclusion by certain Member States of the ESM, the STACOG Treaties and the ESM Framework Agreement.

In the Pringle judgment, the Court of Justice confirmed the possibility for Member States to act in the field of the economic pillar of the EMU by concluding international agreements. In this respect, the Court stated that the new provision amending Article 136 TFEU is not to be considered as the legal basis for the conclusion of the ESM. Indeed, in para 72 of the judgment the Court pointed out that Article 136 para 3 TFEU "confirms" that Member States have the power to establish the stability mechanism.[3] The use of the term "confirm" indicates clearly that the Member States could act unilaterally by the conclusion of an international agreement in the field of economic assistance.

This approach could be used in the future (simplified revision procedure, Article 48 para 6 TEU and modification of Article 136 TFEU) in order to put in place all the necessary legal instruments for the establishment of the Banking Union as a whole. For instance, the conclusion of an agreement to put in place a European resolution system could be envisaged. However, at this stage the Pringle judgment gives only an indication that within the economic pillar the Member State could act unilaterally for the conclusion of an agreement to strengthen their cooperation. The result of such cooperation is to be considered, in the middle run, as European law acquis, as was the case with the Schengen agreement.

Secondly, one of the main questions that the judgment leaves open is how the ESM Treaty, placed outside the EU framework, could be democratically controlled[4] at EU level, which is all the more important when the Court expressly stated that no argumentation could be drawn from the Charter. In this respect, the Court gave a formal answer ensuring the conformity of the ESM with the Charter but lost the occasion to develop a structured reasoning concerning the application of the Charter also in the framework of the conclusion by the Member States of an international agreement

Finally, the Court tried with emphasis to develop for the first time a new reasoning in a field in which there is no case law and for which a specific expertise is required. It is not by chance that in the economic and monetary domain the parties involved, even at a national level, preferred an arbitration system with

---

[2] See in that respect Louis (2006), pp 118–121 and de Witte (2001), p 245.

[3] In that respect and before this judgment some authors pointed out "the declaratory value" of the new Article 136 para 3 TFEU. De Gregorio Merino (2012), pp 1613–1646, sp. 1629 and Borger (2013), pp 113–140, sp. 132. Certain authors have reluctances about the need to amend Article 136 TFEU for the reason that the ESM is established outside the EU law. See in this respect Sester (2012), pp 156–178, sp. 170.

[4] Editorial Comments, Debt and Democracy: United States then, Europe now? (2012) in CMLRev, 1833–1840, p 1835.

experts rather than the traditional judicial model of justice, of which the Court is indisputably a part. Certainly, the Court has demonstrated in the past its power to participate to the elaboration of the EU legal order. However, the issues related to the EMU and in the future to the Banking Union are not limited to a classic legal analysis, for which the Court has the necessary expertise, but have other applications, notably economic, audit, and political which require a specific expertise that today is not ensured by the traditional judicial system put in place via the European Union judicature

Following its legal expertise, the Court developed an important case law in the field of indirect taxation and in the last 10 years in the field of direct taxation. In that respect, it must be recalled that the Court established its case law in the field of direct taxation on the basis of the fundamental principles which govern the common market, namely the free movement of persons, establishment and capital. For the Court it was natural to develop its case law in the field of taxation policy by reference to the fundamental principles governing the so-called "common market". However, the issues related to the economic policy development demonstrated that it was necessary to act also outside the formal framework of the EU Treaties. For this reason, a permanent reference to the case law on concerning the establishment of the common market was not the best solution in order to face the new issues resulting from the evolution of the European Union legal framework.

In the Pringle case, the Court did not have the wish and in any case the time[5] to develop a new case law without referring to its previous judicial standards. Indeed, in a similar context, as was the case for the taxation policy litigation, the Court once again based its reasoning on its case law which, given the completely new and unprecedented context of the Pringle case, proved its limits. The lack of an autonomous economic reasoning by the Court proves the limitedness of this approach. The Court audaciously tried to develop some key concepts concerning the monetary policy and some argumentations such as the financial support on the primary and secondary market. By doing so, it inevitably took a risk to be contested by the experts in the field.

The new competence conferred on the Court on the basis of Article 273 TFEU via the ESM Treaty, the EFSF Framework Agreement and the STACOG Treaty demonstrates that the disputes in the framework of these treaties have a specific nature. Obviously, to solve such sensitive cases as those relating to Member State budgetary discipline or the financial assistance, it is not enough to ensure the effective application of the rules via a judicial system. A debate about the possibility to establish a new specialized jurisdiction on top of the current institutional framework—as is the case in some Member States, e.g. Germany—Bundesfinanzhof—could be started.

Today, at European level, the particular competence in this specific field is conferred on the CJEU on the basis of Article 273 TFEU by the three international agreements (ESM, STACOG, EFSF Framework Agreement). However, the question is whether the CJEU, in this context, can continue to act as a financial judge.

---

[5] The judgment was issued less than 4 months after the reference for a preliminary ruling.

For the moment, the Member States decided to confer this competence on the CJEU for the main reason that the CJEU is considered as the institution which, by its case law, has demonstrated, specifically in the past, consistence and a very sensitive approach on the issues raised during the evolution of the EU law. After the Pringle judgment, the question is whether the Member States will continue to entrust the Court of Justice with this role. The answer to this question is crucial because in addition to the pending litigation before the European Union judicature (i.e. oversight policy and eligibility of marketable debt instruments issued or fully guaranteed by the Hellenic Republic) the current project of the Banking Union, in particular the supervision mechanism, and the European resolution funds require that the competent judicial organ to its legal expertise must be an appropriate financial expert.

References

Borger V (2013) The ESM and the European Court's Predicament in Pringle. GLJ, 113-140

de Gregorio Merino A (2012) Legal Developments in the Economic and Monetary Union during the debt crisis: the mechanism of Financial assistance. CMLRev, 1613–1646

Isaac G (1992) Droit Communautaire Général, 3 edn. Masson, Paris

Louis J.-V. (2006) L'Europe. Sortir du doute. Bruylant, Bruxelles, pp 118-121

Sester P (2012) The ECB's Controversial Securities Market Programme (SMP) and its role in relation to the modified EFSF and the future ESM. ECFLR, 156–178

de Witte B (2001) Chameleonic Member States: differentiation by means of partial and parallel agreements. In: de Witte B, Hanf D, Vos E (eds) The many faces of differentiation in EU law, Intersentia, Anvers

MIX
Papier aus verantwortungsvollen Quellen
Paper from responsible sources
FSC® C105338

If you have any concerns about our products,
you can contact us on
ProductSafety@springernature.com

In case Publisher is established outside the EU,
the EU authorized representative is:
Springer Nature Customer Service Center GmbH
Europaplatz 3, 69115 Heidelberg, Germany

Printed by Libri Plureos GmbH
in Hamburg, Germany